Stay insane,

CRAZY FROM THE HEAT

DAVE'S INSANITY COOKBOOK

Dave Hirschkop
with Kjeld Peterson

TEN SPEED PRESS
Berkeley / Toronto

Ten Speed Press
P.O. Box 7123
Berkeley, California 94707
www.tenspeed.com

Distributed in Australia by Simon and Schuster Australia, in Canada by Ten Speed Press Canada, in New Zealand by Southern Publishers Group, in South Africa by Real Books, and in the United Kingdom and Europe by Airlift Book Company.

Cover and text design by Betsy Stromberg

Library of Congress Cataloging-in-Publication Data
Hirschkop, Dave, 1967–
  Crazy from the heat : Dave's insanity cookbook / Dave Hirschkop with Kjeld Peterson.
    p. cm.
    Includes index.
  ISBN 1-58008-190-8 (pbk.)
    1. Cookery (Hot pepper sauces) I. Peterson, Kjeld. II. Title.
  TX819.H66 H57 2003
  641.8'14—dc21   2003001098

First printing, 2003
Printed in Canada

1 2 3 4 5 6 7 8 9 10 — 07 06 05 04 03

Acknowledgments

This is really is an offbeat compilation of facts and tasty information from a number of valuable people. Without all of these people's support and input, this book would not exist.

I would like to thank Dennis Hayes at Ten Speed Press for having the idea to create this book and the perseverance to convince me that it was a good idea. Meghan Keeffe, also at Ten Speed, was invaluable in taking a rough text and making it into an actual cookbook. Also, I would like to thank all of the people behind the scenes at Ten Speed for pulling this project together and putting this book on a shelf near you.

Kjeld Petersen, who is a talented chef and cooking instructor, was critical with his numerous contributions to the book including a number of great recipes. John Bauccio, who is a creative young culinary wizard and a good writer, was a great help with his wit and ideas.

Of course, my staff at Dave's Gourmet keeps the sauce rolling out the door and supports my ability to participate in projects like this book.

Most of all I would like to thank my wife Paige, who keeps me from needing my straitjacket all the time. In addition, I would like to thank my kids, Emma and Ethan, just for being and my parents for their love and support.

Finally, I would like to thank all of the chileheads and customers who have allowed me to give up my dreams of an undistinguished career counting paper clips for the Bureau of Statistics.

Preface

I never saw it, but I'm sure it was there: an invisible line that somehow surrounded my house as a child. It was a boundary that no chile could ever cross. Chiles were a thing to fear. They were little pieces of evil that I often found in my Chinese food and promptly removed. If only I could reclaim those mild years, interrupted only by the occasional wasabi overdose.

It took a move to California to end that period of my life and teach me that there is more. San Francisco's amazing variety of spicy ethnic food is head spinning: Mexican, Cajun, Thai, Chinese, Indian, and so many more. I tasted some of these cuisines and was hooked. In an effort to spread the word about these delicious foods (especially Mexican), I went back East to the Washington, D.C., area and opened a taqueria called Burrito Madness. Our location at the University of Maryland seemed to attract an unusual variety of pest: college studenticus really drunkicus. In order to rid my restaurant of this vermin, I started creating incendiary sauces.

Like moths to a flame, these mongrels came and burned their faces off. The unusual part is that some of them liked it and wanted it for home use. This was my discovery of the chileheads: a cultlike group, without a secret handshake or a requirement to give up material possessions, but forever bonded by their intense love of the pod.

The chileheads have supported my company, Dave's Gourmet, and our fiery and not-so-fiery sauces for over a decade. This book is for those chileheads and for those who one day may become chileheads. Through this book, I hope to share my knowledge of and passion for chiles and the many ways they can be enjoyed in cooking. What I have learned about the wonderful properties of the pod, so hopefully will others—because mild is a four-letter word.

Contents

Introduction

The story of Dave's Gourmet, and in turn, Insanity Sauce isn't really a story at all. It's more like a journey—a journey that started long ago, and one that travels right over the taste buds of fire-loving tongues all around the world today, and will continue to blaze its trail for years to come. You see, to truly tell the Insanity tale we must begin somewhere in the Americas, about seven thousand (or more) years ago. Long before we had haute cuisine and fancy restaurants, in the part of the world we now call Bolivia and southern Mexico, the folks were trying to find food. They most likely saw some birds eating a wonderfully bright and cheerful-looking fruit, and figured that if the birds could eat it, it must be safe. What the people found, after eating the waxy wonder, was not just a new kind of food, but also one as hot as their long summer days. They had discovered chiles, and we can only guess they were as addictive then as they are today.

Well, the days wore on, and people came and went, and each time they took something back home with them. Eventually, these little brightly colored pods made it to other countries—places with their own cuisines and their own traditions. The only thing missing from these cuisines was a little kick. Oh, sure, they had flavor; we would never dispute the power of garlic and ginger and black pepper and many other exciting ingredients. They just needed something to help wake up their taste buds a little.

The fire grew and, as fires do, it spread very quickly. By the early 1500s, the Portuguese were running the lucrative spice trade out of India, and they brought the chile peppers with them. The places with long-existing traditions of flavor were the first to embrace the chile. Asians added it to their stir-fries, Indians ground it into their curries and chutneys, Africans tossed some in their stews, and

Sicilians knew they were onto something, but until the tomatoes started showing up, they weren't sure what yet.

As the established spice trade routes added chiles, a strange thing happened: people started trying, with some great successes, to grow the plants for themselves. This is what really rooted the chile in the local cuisines. Soon chiles spread to Nepal and into China, through Pakistan and the Middle East, and back around to Eastern Europe. The world now knew what they knew all along in the Americas. Food would never be the same again. Each place along the way seemed to adopt a particular type of chile, which would meld into their culture and food. This transformation was so thorough that even today there are people who are surprised to learn that Thailand, a country in which the average citizen is known to eat almost twice as many chiles as people from anywhere else in the world, did not always have them in its local cuisine.

The funny thing is, that by the time we had fifty states, this new country, so near to the birthplace of all this heat, had no idea what was happening in the little pockets of ethnic cuisines right under the forefathers' noses. There were a few willing to venture into the wonderful restaurants and kitchens that cooked these exciting dishes from exotic locales, but they never seemed to make it out alive.

This brings us to the early 1990s and a little burrito joint called Burrito Madness near the University of Maryland. I was the guy behind the counter, and my little restaurant was inundated with drunken college students who stayed out way past their bedtimes. When I realized that, in order to get them to go home, I had to drive them away, I didn't rest until I had a surefire recipe to get the job done. The restaurant was known for some wonderful salsas and hot sauces, and while these were full of flavor, they never sent anyone home screaming for their mommies. Then one day, after combing the halls of food purveyors and every type of ethnic store I could find, I stumbled across an industrial flavor enhancer—one that, with only a few drops, could change a man's (or at least a drunk frat kid's) life forever.

The stuff was called oleoresin capsicum. And as I would soon find out, oleoresin used improperly was kind of like a liquid form of all the evil in the world. But used in specific formulations, with laboratory-accurate measurements, this stuff could forever change the face of hot sauce and, with it, the eating habits of almost everyone along the way. I immediately recognized the enormity of this discovery and knew that I must wield such power wisely. And so Insanity Sauce was born.

Since I had figured out how to scare the kids back into the dorms only to awaken with a strange craving to return to Burrito Madness, I decided to go out on a new adventure. In 1993, I sold the restaurant and began making and distributing my newest, hottest sauce. At first, no one knew what to do with it. I was banned from the Fiery Foods Show for bringing something that was too spicy. People used traditional hot sauces, and a few even sprinkled a little chile powder on their eggs, but no one had any idea what to make of this stuff. Every day the word was getting out, and suddenly people started getting curious about chiles. There were posters in gourmet food shops and kitchen supply stores chronicling the chile pepper. Folks bought chile *ristras* from farm stands in southern California. Florists even started popping a few into their arrangements. As people started getting curious about Asian, Indian, African, Mexican, and southern Italian cuisines, they noticed a common thread: the chile pepper.

Chiles can really make a meal interesting. They come in dozens of shapes, colors, and flavors. They add that wonderful zing, which can be increased to become a full endorphin experience. They are also extremely healthy—in fact, compared to other foods that people crave, chiles are the best. Chiles have no cholesterol, are low in fat and calories, and have no harmful chemicals like caffeine or alcohol. In addition, eating chiles will make you cool. I mean literally, they actually will cool you down. Why do you think so many people in hot climates are eating chiles?

And so I present *Crazy from the Heat*. After you've made a couple of these recipes, you'll understand what those folks did seven thousand years ago: once you've sampled the food of the chileheads, you'll never go back to living a life without the friendly fire of every bird's favorite fruit.

These recipes come with the same warning as my hot sauces: "This product may be addictive for those with taste buds." In case you want to ease into your addiction (wimp!), pay attention to the heat ratings provided with each recipe:

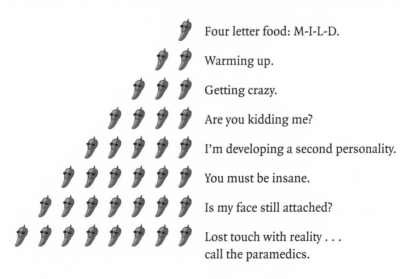

Four letter food: M-I-L-D.

Warming up.

Getting crazy.

Are you kidding me?

I'm developing a second personality.

You must be insane.

Is my face still attached?

Lost touch with reality . . .
call the paramedics.

First Fire

Blazin' Mary
Bloody Mary   7

Smokin' Bean Circles
Spicy Black Bean Tostadas   8

Shoo My Guests out of the House
Spicy Shu Mai Dim Sum   9

Asian Tuna Bombs
Ahi Tartare with Spicy Sesame
Sauce   10

My Aching Muscles
Sake-Steamed Mussels   12

**You're up to Your Dumpling
in Hot Water**
Pot Stickers in a Hot Pot   13

Smokin' in the Beans Room
Chipotle Bean Dip   14

**My Chicken's Cooked and
My Nuts Are Roasting**
Chicken Satay with Spicy Peanut
Sauce   15

Martian Mole
Spicy Guacamole   16

Hurtin' Jalapeño Poppers
Jalapeño Cheese Poppers   17

Kamikaze Rolls
Chile-Stuffed Chun Guen
Spring Rolls   18

Fiery Fritters
Crab 'n Corn Fritters   19

Cherry Drums
Ancho-Cherry Chicken Drumettes   20

Pita Piper's Peck of Peppers
Muhammara (Pepper Dip)   21

A Crab's Birthday Cake
Jalapeño Crab Cakes   22

Crustacean Sensation
Crab-Stuffed Jalapeño Boats   23

Dip on the Wild Side
Chipotle Cheese Fondue   24

A Chip off the Old Tuna
Sesame Tuna with Won Ton Chips
and Salsa   25

Rolling in the Onion Patch
Spicy Asian Chicken and
Scallion Rolls   26

Piggy Pie
Spicy Pork Empanadas   27

Acid Fish
Ceviche with Chile Crackers   28

Blazin' Mary
Bloody Mary

If you're tired of those bland Bloody Marys from major manufacturers or from timid bartenders, stand up for your rights. Demand some heat; demand some horseradish; demand some black pepper—and demand it now. A good Bloody Mary is not just a drink; it is a sauce for shrimp, it is a soup, and it is a bath (if you get sprayed by a skunk). The award-winning mix that I make, Insane Mary Mix, is all of that and more (a shameless plug). You can also add a dash of Worcestershire and a pinch of black pepper to this recipe if you like.

Serves 6   Prep time: 10 minutes

Heat rating: (with Insanity Sauce)

- 1 tablespoon freshly squeezed lemon juice
- 1 tablespoon freshly squeezed lime juice
- 1/2 teaspoon finely minced lemon zest
- 1/2 teaspoon finely minced lime zest
- 1 dried chipotle chile, stemmed, seeded, and finely chopped
- 1 fresh red Fresno chile, stemmed, seeded, and finely chopped
- 1 teaspoon sugar

- 3 cups tomato juice
- 1 teaspoon ground cumin
- Pinch of celery salt
- 2 drops Insanity Sauce (optional)
- 2/3 cup ice-cold vodka (store your vodka in the freezer, and you'll always be ready!)
- 6 celery stalks with leaves, for garnish
- 6 fresh red chiles of your choice, for garnish

Muddle together the lemon and lime juices and zests, chiles, and sugar in a mortar and pestle. Pour into a pitcher, add the tomato juice, and stir in the cumin, celery salt, and Insanity Sauce. Stir in the vodka and pour into tall glasses filled with ice.

Prepare each garnish by spearing a chile and a celery stalk together using a toothpick. Insert one into each glass and serve. The chile will be fair warning to anyone involved with your festivities.

Capsaicin has been shown to help with postsurgical and chronic pain, and with mouth pain in chemotherapy patients. It is also used in creams for shingles and arthritis.

Smokin' Bean Circles
Spicy Black Bean Tostadas

Long ago these mysterious circles were found in the culinary field. Their delicious flavor, however, has never been explained. This is the type of dish that I loved back in my days of Mexican cooking. Although, you can get away with Cheddar or Jack, use the Mexican queso cotija or the feta, and you will taste the difference.

Serves 8   Prep time: 20 minutes

Heat rating:

1 tablespoon vegetable oil
1 yellow onion, diced
1 green bell pepper, seeded and diced
1 tablespoon ground cumin
3 tablespoons Cool Cayenne Pepper Sauce or other Louisiana-style hot sauce
4 cups canned black beans
1/2 teaspoon salt
1 cup sour cream
1 1/2 tablespoons Jump Up and Kiss Me Smoky Chipotle Sauce or puréed canned chipotle chiles in adobo sauce

16 (4-inch) corn tortillas, wrapped in foil and warmed in a 350°F oven for 10 minutes
Torn lettuce, for garnish
Chopped tomatoes, for garnish
Queso cotija or any Mexican cheese or mild feta that can be crumbled, for garnish
Sliced avocados, for garnish

Heat the oil in a saucepan and sauté the onion and pepper until soft. Add the cumin, pepper sauce, beans, and salt and cook until the beans are heated through. In a small bowl, mix the sour cream and chipotle sauce. To assemble each tostada, spoon a line of chipotle sour cream down the center of the tortilla, and add 1/4 cup of the bean mixture. Top with garnishes and serve. You can also fry the tortillas in oil and eat them crispy.

Apparently it is hip to be smoky and the chipotle's popularity is smokin'. When buying chipotles (dried smoked jalapeños), understand that there are many kinds. Mainly there is the darker chipotle that is made from a green jalapeño and the morita, or mora, made from a jalapeño that has been allowed to ripen to red. You will usually find chipotles either dried or canned in adobo (tomato sauce).

Shoo My Guests out of the House
Spicy Shu Mai Dim Sum

If you've ever had dim sum, and especially shu mai, you won't want to share. Get those mooching neighbors out of your house and *bon appétit*. I love these guys dipped in spicy mustard or a piquant Asian sauce. Look for won ton skins in the refrigerated section of Asian markets or in the Asian section of most supermarkets.

Serves 4   **Prep time: 45 minutes**

Heat rating:

FILLING
- 1 tablespoon peanut or vegetable oil
- 1 tablespoon peeled finely minced fresh gingerroot
- 1 tablespoon finely minced garlic
- 3 fresh Thai or jalapeño chiles, stemmed, seeded, and finely minced
- 1 shallot, finely minced
- 1/2 cup mirin
- 6 sprigs cilantro, leaves only, finely chopped
- 1 pound precooked boneless chicken, pork, beef, or seafood, finely minced
- 1 egg
- 1 tablespoon water
- 16 won ton skins
- Green onions, green part only, thinly chopped, for garnish

To make the filling, heat the oil in sauté pan over medium heat. Add the ginger, garlic, chiles, and shallot. Sauté for 3 to 4 minutes without coloring. Carefully deglaze the pan with the mirin and continue cooking over medium heat until almost dry, about 5 minutes. Transfer to a bowl, add the cilantro and meat or seafood, and stir to combine. Cover and refrigerate to cool.

In a small bowl, whisk the egg with the water. Using a small pastry brush, lightly brush 1 of the won ton skins around the edge with the egg mixture. Place 2 tablespoons of the cooled filling in the center of the skin and draw up all four corners to the top to form a pyramid shape, making sure that all edges are sealed by firmly grasping each of the four edges and pulling toward the top. Repeat with the remaining wrappers and filling.

Using a bamboo or rice steamer, steam the assembled dim sum gently for 3 to 5 minutes or until heated through. Alternatively, using a pot with a steam rack, place 1 to 2 inches of water in the pot and bring to a slow boil. Place the dim sum on the rack over the boiling water, cover, and steam accordingly. Garnish with the green onions.

Dim sum is a deliciously varied type of Chinese finger food, usually served in tea houses. In Cantonese *dim sum* means "touching your heart." Dim sum also happens to be just the right size for throwing and would be my first choice in a food fight.

Asian Tuna Bombs
Ahi Tartare with Spicy Sesame Sauce

Who says that war is hell? You'll *want* to face a full-scale bombing of these delicious appetizers. This dish is tangy and light, with an explosion of flavor.

Serves 4   **Prep time: 20 minutes, plus refrigerator time**

Heat rating:

1 pound fresh ahi tuna, cut into
    ¹/₂-inch dice
2 teaspoons salt
¹/₄ teaspoon ground white pepper
2 tablespoons minced yellow onion
4 sprigs parsley, leaves only, finely minced
1 tablespoon Dijon mustard
Juice of 2 lemons

¹/₄ cup olive oil
1 fresh Thai or red jalapeño chile,
    stemmed, seeded, and finely minced
Water crackers, for serving
1 ¹/₂ cups Spicy Sesame Sauce
    (recipe follows)
Sesame seeds, for garnish
Thinly sliced green onion, for garnish

Place the tuna in a medium mixing bowl, season with the salt and pepper, and set aside. In a small mixing bowl, combine the onion, parsley, mustard, lemon juice, oil, and chile, whisking until smooth. Pour the vinaigrette over the tuna and refrigerate, covered, for a minimum of 1 hour and up to 24 hours.

To serve, place crackers on a serving platter and top with spoonfuls of tuna, allowing the marinade to dribble on the crackers. Drizzle the tuna and chips with the sesame sauce and garnish with the sesame seeds and green onions. Bombs away.

"Ahi" is the Hawaiin name for yellowfin tuna. These guys can reach three hundred pounds and pack a ton of flavor. Don't confuse them with the huge bluefin tuna that are used to make sushi; the flesh of the yellowfin is generally much paler than the bluefin's deep red flesh.

SPICY SESAME SAUCE

Makes 1 ¹/₂ cups   **Prep time: 10 minutes**

Heat rating:

¹/₄ cup toasted sesame oil
1 cup soy sauce
3 tablespoons sesame seeds, toasted
1 tablespoon crushed red chile flakes
1 teaspoon Garlic-Chile Sauce or Asian
   garlic-chile paste

1 teaspoon salt
¹/₂ teaspoon ground white pepper
1 green onion, white part only, very thinly
   sliced

To prepare the sauce, combine all of the ingredients in a small saucepan and bring to a simmer over medium heat. Lower the heat to very low and continue to cook until reduced by a third, about 5 minutes. Strain the sauce while still warm and cool to room temperature before using.

Sesame oils really vary. You might want to be careful with underroasted American and Chinese brands that are bland. The Japanese oils tend to have a stronger flavor. You can usually tell by how aromatic it is. In general, Asian oils are darker and more intense in flavor.

My Aching Muscles
Sake-Steamed Mussels

You smell the steam. Your mouth waters. Your muscles burn. Still, you push yourself. Why? Because they taste so good. Before long you have finished all twenty-four. Or if you don't finish them, call me, I'll eat them. This is a great appetizer or light meal—perfect for a brunch. Serve these with really good French bread and a nice white wine. Dashi is a light Japanese fish stock that can be found in Asian markets or in the Asian section of some supermarkets.

Serves 6   **Prep time: 30 minutes**

Heat rating:

24 mussels, scrubbed well
2 tablespoons chopped green onions
2 cloves garlic, chopped
2 teaspoons Garlic-Chile Sauce or Asian garlic-chile paste
1 pinch shichimi (see sidebar; optional)

1 teaspoon chopped fresh parsley
$^1/_4$ cup sake
$^1/_2$ cup dashi or lightly salted water
4 tablespoons butter
Sliced French bread, for serving

Combine the mussels, green onions, garlic, Garlic-Chile Sauce, shichimi, parsley, sake, dashi, and butter in a large, heavy-bottomed sauté pan. Cover and place over high heat until all of the shells have opened, about 5 minutes. Discard any mussels that have not opened.

To serve as an appetizer, place the mussels and broth in a serving bowl and serve with slices of French bread for dipping in the broth. To serve as an entrée, place a thick slice of bread or a mound of rice in the bottom of individual bowls and divide the mussels and broth equally over the top.

Shichimi, sometimes called "seven spice," is a Japanese condiment made up of chile flakes (togarahi), sansho (a type of pepper, not chile, unique to Japan and China), white poppy seeds, white sesame seeds, black hemp seeds, dried mandarin orange peel, and nori (seaweed) flakes. It's available in Asian markets. If you find different strengths, go for the hot.

You're up to Your Dumpling in Hot Water

Pot Stickers in a Hot Pot

Shabu-shabu (Japanese hot pot) is incredible; I eat it all the time. A pot of hot broth is put on the table and you cook the fresh ingredients right in front of you. It makes a great dinner party; if the guests don't like the food, they'll have no one to blame but themselves! In addition to pot stickers, you can put thinly sliced pieces of fish, chicken, meat, veggies, or almost anything in the hot pot. Garnishes and sauces can be hot mustard dip, ponzu sauce, plum sauce, more Garlic-Chile Sauce, and Asian garlic-chile paste.

Serves 4   **Prep time: 45 minutes, plus refrigerator time**

Heat rating:

1 tablespoon vegetable oil
1 pound boneless chicken breast meat, cut into 1-inch cubes
2 small fresh red chiles (such as Thai or serrano), stemmed, seeded, and very finely minced
16 pot sticker wrappers or won ton skins
1 egg, lightly beaten
4 cups chicken stock or broth

1 small head Chinese or napa cabbage, cut into bite-size pieces
1 bunch spinach, thoroughly rinsed and stemmed
4 ounces firm tofu, cut into small cubes (about 1/2 cup)
1/4 pound button or brown mushrooms, thinly sliced

In a sauté pan over medium heat, heat the oil. Add the chicken and cook, stirring occasionally, until no longer pink in the center. Transfer to a cutting board, let cool, then mince. Combine the chicken with the chiles in a bowl.

Prepare the pot sticker wrappers by unwrapping them and laying them in a single layer on a flat work surface. Brush one edge of each wrapper lightly with the egg and place about 2 tablespoons of the chicken mixture in the middle of each wrapper. Fold the wrapper over the filling and secure the ends together using additional egg if necessary, setting each aside until all of the wrappers are filled.

Arrange the cabbage, spinach, tofu, and mushrooms on a serving platter.

Heat the stock in a saucepan until gently boiling. Reduce the heat to a simmer. Place the hot pot in the center of the table over a small, portable heat source. Surround it with small individual plates of the pot stickers and serve along with the vegetables. Guests will take pot stickers and/or vegetables and float them in the hot pot until just heated through, removing hopefully only their own selections to their serving bowl.

Smokin' in the Beans Room
Chipotle Bean Dip

This is why they invented tortilla chips. Actually, forget the tortilla chips. Lock yourself in your bedroom and eat the whole bowl of dip with your hands. Don't forget to lick your fingers. Epazote is a fresh herb said to reduce the gassiness of beans; here, it doesn't contribute much flavor.

Serves 3   **Prep time: 15 minutes, plus cooking and soaking**

Heat rating: **(with Insanity Sauce)**

1 pound dried beans (pinto or black), rinsed

1 sprig epazote (optional)

3 tablespoons vegetable oil or lard

1 (4-ounce) can chipotle chiles in adobo sauce

1/4 cup tomato sauce

1 clove garlic, peeled

1 yellow onion, coarsely chopped

1 tablespoon achiote (annatto) paste (optional)

1/2 cup freshly squeezed orange juice

6 fresh red serrano chiles, stemmed, seeded, and minced

1 drop Insanity Sauce (optional)

1 bunch cilantro, leaves only

1 1/2 tablespoons vegetable or corn oil

2 teaspoons salt

1/2 teaspoon freshly ground black pepper

Sort through the beans and check for pebbles and things that could break a tooth—we want to protect those teeth and taste buds so we can properly burn them later in the book.

Place the beans in a deep soup pot and cover with water. Allow the beans to soak overnight. Drain and refill the pot with fresh water, enough to cover the beans, and add the epazote. Bring the beans to a boil, then lower the heat and allow the beans to simmer, covered, for 1 to 1 1/2 hours, or until they are soft. (Add additional hot water to the pot during the cooking time if needed to prevent burning, until the beans are fully cooked). Drain any water left in the pot. In a large sauté pan (an iron skillet is perfect, if you have one), heat the oil over medium heat and add the beans to the pan to "refry" them. Stir the beans constantly, mashing them slightly while frying them, taking care not to scorch the beans on the bottom of the pan. Cool and reserve.

Place the chipotles with their sauce, tomato sauce, garlic, onion, achiote, orange juice, chiles, Insanity Sauce, cilantro, vegetable oil, salt, and pepper into the bowl of food processor and process until smooth and thick, adding more oil to the mixture, if needed, to thin to the desired consistency. Fold the chipotle mixture into the beans, heat together over low heat until warmed through, and serve.

To make this much thinner and use it as a sauce on grilled chicken or pork chops for example, double the amount of orange juice and tomato sauce, and definitely add at least 1 tablespoon of additional oil when processing.

My Chicken's Cooked and My Nuts Are Roasting
Chicken Satay with Spicy Peanut Sauce

Why does every Thai restaurant menu have this dish on it? Because it's great, silly! This version packs a *muy* Thai punch. A traditional accompaniment is a sweet pickled cucumber salad.

Serves 4   **Prep time: 1 hour**

Heat rating: **(with Insanity Sauce)**

SPICY PEANUT SAUCE
2 tablespoons vegetable or peanut oil
2 green onions, white part only, finely chopped
1 clove garlic, finely chopped
1 tablespoon peeled and finely ground fresh gingerroot
1/4 cup distilled white vinegar
3 tablespoons firmly packed light brown sugar
1/4 cup soy sauce
1/4 teaspoon crushed red pepper flakes
1/2 cup creamy peanut butter
1 cup water
1 drop Insanity Sauce (optional)

SATAY
1 pound boneless skinless chicken breast halves
1 teaspoon minced garlic
2 tablespoons freshly squeezed lime juice
1 tablespoon firmly packed light brown sugar
1 tablespoon peeled grated fresh gingerroot, or 1 teaspoon galangal powder
1/2 teaspoon turmeric
Pinch of ground coriander
Pinch of ground cumin
Pinch of salt

Sliced serrano chiles, for garnish
Diced red onion, for garnish

To prepare the sauce, heat the oil over medium heat in a saucepan until hot. Cook the green onions, garlic, and ginger about 1 minute, stirring constantly. Mix in the vinegar, brown sugar, soy sauce, pepper flakes, peanut butter, and water and bring to a simmer, still stirring. Simmer the sauce, stirring, until smooth (say that ten times really fast), 2 to 3 minutes. Cool to room temperature. Add a dash of Insanity Sauce for some real heat. If the sauce is too thick for your liking, add small amounts of hot water until it's the right consistency. (You can make the sauce a day or two ahead of time; to store, cover and refrigerate, then bring to room temperature before using.)

To prepare the satay, cut the chicken across the grain into 4-inch strips and place them in a large, shallow pan. Blend the remaining satay ingredients together in a small bowl. Pour over the chicken and let marinate for 30 minutes, tossing frequently. Meanwhile, soak 12 6-inch wooden skewers in water so they don't burn during cooking.

Prepare a fire in a charcoal grill, preheat a gas grill to medium heat, or preheat the broiler. Thread the chicken onto the wooden skewers. Grill or broil until browned, about 5 minutes. Serve the skewers hot, garnished with the chiles and onion, with the peanut sauce alongside.

Martian Mole
Spicy Guacamole

This is either the first recipe from another planet or maybe it just tastes out of this world. Guacamole is just a way of showcasing the great flavor of avocado. I love this recipe but if you want a creamier guacamole, add some of the optional mayonnaise. For a hybrid flavor you can mix this with a $1/2$ cup of your favorite salsa.

Serves 4   **Prep time: 15 minutes**

Heat rating: 🌶 🌶 🌶 🌶 🌶 **(with Insanity Sauce)**

2 large ripe avocados, peeled and pitted
4 teaspoons freshly squeezed lime juice
$1/2$ cup chopped fresh cilantro
$1/2$ cup finely chopped white onion
1 large tomato, cut into $1/4$-inch dice
4 large cloves garlic, finely chopped
4 large fresh serrano chiles, seeded and chopped

$1/2$ teaspoon salt
$1/2$ teaspoon freshly ground black pepper
1 to 2 drops Insanity Sauce, or for the brave, Ultimate Insanity Sauce (optional)
1 to 2 tablespoons mayonnaise (optional)

Using a fork, mash the avocado with the lime juice in a small bowl. Add the cilantro, onion, tomato, garlic, chiles, salt, pepper, and Insanity Sauce and stir to combine. For a super-creamy guacamole, add the mayonnaise. Helpful hint: don't use this for facial packs, as it might be painful. If not serving immediately, tightly cover. You can also add some lemon juice to prevent discoloration.

Don't read this if you are going to make this dish. The avocado is a fruit whose name comes from the Nahuatl Indian word for "testicle." This may make those Rocky Mountain oyster eaters hungry, but I prefer the avocado's early name: alligator pear. By the way, putting the pit in the guacamole to maintain color is a myth.

Hurtin' Jalapeño Poppers
Jalapeño Cheese Poppers

You will want to pop these tasty treats into your mouth because they taste so good; your eyes will pop open because of the zip. For you experimental types, you can apply the idea of turducken (a stuffed hen stuffed into a duck which is then stuffed into a turkey) to this recipe: Stuff a chile pequín into your jalapeño poppers and pop the popper into a New Mexico chile and then roll and cook.

Serves 4   **Prep time: 30 minutes**

Heat rating:

¹/₄ cup all-purpose flour
1 ¹/₂ cups Ritz cracker crumbs
1 teaspoon salt
1 large egg

2 ounces firm cream cheese or Monterey Jack cheese
12 fresh jalapeños
Vegetable or corn oil, for deep-frying

Mix together the flour, cracker crumbs, and salt in a shallow dish. In a separate dish, beat the egg. Cut the cheese into 1 by ¹/₂ by ¹/₄-inch cubes. Cut 1 ¹/₂-inch slits lengthwise along both sides of each jalapeño.

To reduce the heat, you may also open up the chiles a little more and seed and devein them. Insert the cheese into each jalapeño by prying it open. Chill the chiles for about 5 minutes.

Dip the jalapeños in the egg to coat, drip off excess, then roll in flour mixture and shake off excess. Layer on a plate and chill again for 5 minutes. If you have problems getting the coating to stick, first roughen the jalapeño skins with a fork or with a serrated knife.

In a deep frying pan, heat oil to a depth of 2 inches over medium heat until hot, not smoking. Pop your jalapeños into the oil, turning them, for a minute or two, or until golden brown. Transfer with a slotted spoon onto paper towels to drain. Season with salt. Arrange on a serving platter and pop them in your mouth. For even hotter results, try this with habaneros (but we don't take calls from whiners, so beware).

You should always taste test your chiles before throwing them into your recipes; sometimes a jalapeño tastes like a bell pepper, sometimes it is hotter than heck.

Kamikaze Rolls
Chile Stuffed Chun Guen Spring Rolls

Dive into these spring rolls with full fervor—they're crispy, savory, tangy, and awesome. You can also make them with ground pork or chicken. For nongreasy rolls, make sure that your oil is really hot (about 375°F) and that you pat off the excess oil after cooking.

Serves 4 (about 20 spring rolls)   **Prep time: 30 minutes**

Heat rating:

6 medium fresh shiitake mushrooms, stemmed and coarsely chopped

2 cups drained canned water chestnuts, coarsely chopped

8 ounces fresh bean sprouts

3 stalks celery, deribbed and finely chopped

4 fresh green jalapeño chiles, stemmed, seeded, and finely minced

2 tablespoons vegetable oil, plus additional for deep-frying

1 teaspoon Garlic-Chile Sauce or Asian garlic-chile paste, plus additional for serving

1 teaspoon sugar

1 teaspoon salt

20 egg roll skins

1 egg, lightly beaten

Soyabi Sauce or soy sauce, for serving

Rinse the mushrooms, water chestnuts, sprouts, celery, and chiles in cold water. Drain well. Preheat a sauté pan or wok and add the 2 tablespoons oil. Heat until hot, but do not allow it to smoke. Sauté or stir-fry the combined vegetables in the oil until crisp-tender, about 3 to 5 minutes. Add the Garlic-Chile Sauce, sugar, and salt and continue to cook for an additional minute. Remove from the heat and let cool.

Arrange the egg roll skins on a work surface with the points at the top, bottom, right, and left, in a diamond shape. For each roll, place 4 to 5 teaspoons of the filling in the lower section of the skin and fold the bottom portion of the skin up and over the filling. Firmly roll the wrapper up to about half way up the sheet. Moisten the right and left corners with the beaten egg and fold the two sides in over the filling. Continue to roll up and secure the top with additional egg. Set aside on a plate and proceed to assemble the remaining egg rolls.

Preheat the oven to 250°F and line a baking sheet with paper towels.

Heat additional oil to a depth of 2 to 3 inches in a deep pan or wok. Working in batches, deep-fry the spring rolls in the oil until golden brown, turning occasionally, about 2 minutes. Transfer with a slotted spoon to the paper towel–lined baking sheet to drain. Fry the remaining rolls. (The rolls may be made 15 minutes ahead of serving and kept warm in a 250°F oven.)

The rolls may be served hot or at room temperature and can be left whole or cut into a variety of shapes. Serve with additional Garlic-Chile Sauce and the Soyabi Sauce, for dipping.

Fiery Fritters
Crab 'n Corn Fritters

Some people might call these crab cakes, but they don't seem like cake to me. These are definitely fritters and are definitely spicy, not to mention great. Whether you use blue, stone, or Dungeness crab (but not imitation) this dish will have those mooches at your party asking to freeload a little longer, and drinking their way through your bar even faster.

Serves 1 really big guy or 4 normal people (about 20 fritters)

Prep time: 45 minutes

Heat rating: 🌶 🌶 🌶 🌶 🌶 🌶 🌶

1 (11-ounce) can corn niblets, drained and rinsed

8 ounces fresh crabmeat, roughly chopped

2 fresh green Scotch bonnet or habanero chiles, stemmed, seeded, and minced

2 fresh red Fresno, serrano, or jalapeño chiles, stemmed, seeded, and minced

2 small shallots, finely chopped

2 cloves garlic, finely chopped

1 egg, beaten

2 tablespoons water

1/4 cup all-purpose flour

1/4 teaspoon baking soda

1 teaspoon ground cumin

1/2 teaspoon ground coriander

1 teaspoon salt

3 tablespoons canola oil

Lime wedges, for garnish

Blend the corn into a coarse paste in a food processor, but do not purée. Transfer to a bowl and add the crab, chiles, shallots, garlic, egg, and water. Mix well. In another bowl, mix together the flour, baking soda, spices, and salt. Add to the corn mixture and stir gently to combine.

Preheat the oven to 250°F and line a large baking sheet with paper towels.

In a large frying pan over high heat, heat the oil 375°F. Carefully drop large spoonfuls (each one about 2 or 3 tablespoons) of the mixture into the oil until as many have been added as can fit without touching. Fry on each side until golden brown, about 2 minutes total. Using a slotted spoon, transfer to the paper towel–lined baking sheet to drain. Repeat for the remaining fritters. (The fritters may be made 15 minutes ahead of serving and kept warm in a 250°F oven.) Serve hot, garnished with lime wedges.

Even though habaneros and Scotch bonnets belong to the *Chinense* species (*Chinense* could be translated as "being from China"), they are from neither China nor Scotland. Most believe that all chiles originated in either present-day Bolivia or southern Mexico.

Cherry Drums
Ancho-Cherry Chicken Drumettes

I love chicken wings. They are a great American food. The meat is always moist, there is enough skin and fat for maximum flavor, and they taste especially great with this ancho-cherry sauce. You might want to make some extra sauce because darn near everything tastes good with it. For a sauce that is really fiery, add a minced habanero chile to the sauce (bumping the heat rating to 6).

Serves 10   Prep time: 55 minutes

Heat rating:

ANCHO-CHERRY SAUCE
1 1/4 cups apple cider vinegar
3/4 cup ketchup
3/4 cup chopped onion
3/4 cup dried tart cherries
1/3 cup firmly packed dark brown sugar
1/4 cup water
3 tablespoons mild-flavored (light) molasses

2 to 3 large dried ancho chiles (about 1 1/4 ounce), stemmed and seeded
2 cloves garlic
1 teaspoon ground coriander
Pinch of ground cloves
Salt and freshly ground black pepper

3 pounds chicken drumettes or wings

Combine all of the sauce ingredients except salt and pepper in a heavy saucepan. Bring to boil. Reduce the heat to medium-low, cover, and simmer until the chiles and cherries are tender, about 20 minutes. Working in batches, purée the mixture in a blender. Return the sauce to the pan. Simmer uncovered until the sauce is reduced to 3 cups and thickens. Season with salt and pepper to taste. (The sauce can be made up to 2 days in advance. Cover and chill until ready to use.)

Prepare a fire in a charcoal grill or preheat a gas grill to medium heat. Sprinkle the chicken with salt and pepper. Grill until just cooked through, turning occasionally, about 10 minutes. Pour 1 cup of the sauce into a small bowl. Brush some of the sauce over the chicken and continue grilling until glazed, turning and basting with more sauce often, about 5 minutes longer. Serve with the remaining sauce.

Pita Piper's Peck of Peppers
Muhammara (Pepper Dip)

Everyone knows hummus and baba ghanoush, but Middle Easterners having been holding out on us. This is the real thing; real good that is. If you adore chiles, then muhammara must be on your table. Key ingredients are roasted red peppers and pomegranate molasses, a reduction of pomegranate juice available in Middle Eastern markets. Try this Turkish favorite at your next party.

Serves 4   **Prep time: 45 minutes**

Heat rating:

2 red bell peppers, roasted, peeled, stemmed, and seeded
²/₃ cup finely ground fresh bread crumbs
¹/₃ cup walnuts, lightly toasted and finely chopped
3 cloves garlic, minced and mashed to a paste with ¹/₂ teaspoon salt
1 tablespoon freshly squeezed lemon juice

2 teaspoons pomegranate molasses
1 teaspoon ground cumin
¹/₂ teaspoon crushed red pepper flakes
2 tablespoons extra virgin olive oil
Salt
Toasted pita triangles, as an accompaniment

In a food processor, combine the bell peppers, bread crumbs, walnuts, garlic, lemon juice, pomegranate molasses, cumin, and pepper flakes and process until the mixture is smooth. With the motor running, gradually add the oil. Season with the salt to taste. Transfer to a bowl and serve at room temperature, along with the pita triangles. Note: for additional flavor and heat, you can also add 1 tablespoon of balsamic vinegar and/or 1 minced habanero chile.

Toasting nuts and seeds brings out lots of flavor. You can do this on the stove or in the oven. A small sauté pan over medium heat is perfect, and no oil is necessary. Watch the pan closely and keep the nuts or seeds moving. If toasting in the oven, set it for 350°F, and use a baking sheet placed on a middle rack. Shake the pan once in a while and don't forget to watch the nuts or seeds closely. Depending on the nut or seed, it will take from 3 to 10 minutes.

A Crab's Birthday Cake
Jalapeño Crab Cakes

"Handle with care" should be marked on most crab cakes. They can definitely fall apart, especially when they have a lot of lump crabmeat that is not broken up or are not chilled. Crab cakes are great.

Serves 4   **Prep time: 25 minutes, plus chilling time**

Heat rating:

3 tablespoons vegetable oil
1 red bell pepper, seeded and diced small
6 slices white bread, crusts removed, lightly toasted, and torn into pieces
1 pound jumbo lump crabmeat, preferably from blue crabs
1/4 cup chopped fresh cilantro

1/4 cup mayonnaise
1 1/2 tablespoons Old Bay seasoning
1 fresh jalapeño chile, stemmed, seeded, and minced
1 tablespoon minced garlic
Pinch of salt
Pinch of freshly ground black pepper

Heat 1 tablespoon of the oil over moderately high heat until hot but not smoking. Add the bell peppers and sauté until softened, about 5 minutes. Set aside to cool.

In a food processor, grind the bread into fine crumbs (you can also buy prepared bread crumbs). In a bowl, stir together the bell peppers, crab, cilantro, mayonnaise, Old Bay seasoning, chile, garlic, and 2 tablespoons of the breadcrumbs. Season with the salt and pepper. Mix until well combined, cover, and chill 20 minutes.

Divide the crab mixture into 12 equal portions and pat each into 1/2-inch-thick patties (flat on the top and bottom). Spread the remaining bread crumbs on a sheet of wax paper and coat the crab cakes evenly with the crumbs. To help prevent crumbling during cooking, chill the crab cakes, covered loosely, for at least 2 hours before sautéing.

Preheat the oven to 375°F. In a large pan, heat 1 tablespoon of the oil over moderately high heat until hot but not smoking and sauté half of the crab cakes until golden brown on the bottom, 3 to 4 minutes. Turn the crab cakes carefully with a spatula and brown the opposite sides, 3 to 4 minutes. Carefully transfer the sautéed crab cakes to a baking sheet. Add the remaining 1 tablespoon oil to the pan and sauté the remaining crab cakes in same manner, transferring to a baking sheet when browned. Bake the crab cakes in the oven for 5 minutes, or until heated through.

Crustacean Sensation
Crab-Stuffed Jalapeño Boats

It seems a shame that some of the finger foods that you love at parties, you get to enjoy only at parties. This is one of those dishes. It is a great appetizer, snack or party item. One great aspect of this recipe is that it is too spicy to share with the faint of heart, and it can't be toned down. You can also try brushing the jalapeños with olive oil and grilling them, instead of deep-frying in batter.

Serves 4   **Prep time: 1 hour, plus 30 minutes standing time**

Heat rating:  **(with Total Insanity Sauce)**

12 large fresh jalapeño chiles
4 ounces fresh or frozen crabmeat, well drained
1/3 cup minced red onion
1/4 cup minced green bell pepper
1/4 cup plus 1 tablespoon mayonnaise
Pinch of salt, plus additional as needed
Pinch of freshly ground black pepper, plus additional as needed

1/2 cup all-purpose flour, plus additional for dredging
3/4 cup beer
Corn oil, for deep-frying
1/2 avocado, peeled, pitted, and diced
1/2 cup prepared medium-hot salsa, drained in a sieve or colander
2 drops Total Insanity Sauce (optional)

Starting just below the stem, cut the chiles lengthwise in half, leaving the stems attached. Seed the chiles with a spoon and place them in a heavy saucepan. Cover with cold water and bring to a boil; decrease the heat to a simmer, and cook for 2 minutes. Drain. Pat the chiles dry. Set aside.

Combine the crab, onion, bell pepper, and the 1/4 cup mayonnaise in a small bowl. Season with the salt and pepper. Fill the chile cavities with the crab mixture. Press chile halves together to compress filling. (The chiles can be stuffed up to 4 hours in advance. Cover and refrigerate until ready to cook.)

Place 1/2 cup flour in a bowl. Gradually whisk in beer. Let the batter stand 30 minutes.

Preheat the oven to 250°F and line a large baking sheet with paper towels.

Heat 4 inches of corn oil in a deep, heavy pot to 375°F. Whisk the batter until smooth. Dredge the chiles in a shallow dish of flour. Holding the stem, coat with batter completely and deep-fry in batches until golden brown, about 3 minutes. Using a slotted spoon, transfer the chiles to the prepared baking sheet to drain. (The chiles should be kept warm in a 250°F oven until ready to serve.)

Combine the avocado, salsa, and the remaining 1 tablespoon mayonnaise in a small bowl and stir gently. Season with salt and pepper to taste. Put the chiles on a serving platter. Serve with the salsa mixture, spiked with the Total Insanity Sauce, in a bowl alongside.

Dip on the Wild Side
Chipotle Cheese Fondue

Most people either love or hate fondues. They can have a strong flavor and a certain sharpness that I personally don't like. You probably could guess what ingredients I really like in a fondue: the smokiness and bite of the chipotles, the sweetness of the kirsch, and the incredible flavor of the shallots make this dish a real winner.

Serves 8   **Prep time: 25 minutes**

Heat rating:

¹/₄ cup vegetable oil
1 ¹/₂ cups thinly sliced shallots (about 8 large shallots)
Salt
2 cups Gruyère cheese, finely diced
2 cups Emmetaler cheese, finely diced
1 ¹/₂ tablespoons cornstarch

2 large cloves garlic, halved
1 ¹/₃ cups dry white wine
1 tablespoon freshly squeezed lemon juice
1 ¹/₂ tablespoons kirsch
3 drained canned chipotle chiles in adobo sauce, minced
Freshly ground black pepper

Add the oil and shallots to a skillet over medium-high heat and sauté, stirring, until golden brown, about 3 minutes. Transfer the shallots to paper towels to dry and season with salt to taste. Set aside.

In a medium bowl, mix together the cheeses and cornstarch. Rub the inside of a large saucepan with the garlic halves and, leaving the garlic in the pan, add the wine and lemon juice. Bring the liquid just to a boil and gradually stir in the cheese mixture by the handful. Bring the mixture to a low simmer over moderate heat, stirring, and stir in the kirsch, chiles, and pepper to taste. Transfer the fondue to a fondue pot and set over a low flame. Stir in the fried shallots.

Serve with fondue forks or wooden skewers for dipping vegetable and fruit pieces and bread cubes.

Kirsch, German for "cherry," is a brandy that is made from cherries (no surprise there). It is also is similar to my last name, which begins with *Hirsch*, German for "a male deer" (stag).

A Chip off the Old Tuna
Sesame Tuna with Won Ton Chips and Salsa

Maybe I am a little nuts, but I think that there's a conspiracy. Tuna is the stuff that comes in a can, is a little dry, but tastes pretty good with mayonnaise. Ahi, and all this high quality "tuna" nowadays, has to be a different fish. I bet it's the result of a genetic experiment in which scientists crossbred filet mignon with swordfish. Realizing the public would have a problem with this unsavory project, they covered the whole thing up and gave this new fish a different name. Sorry Charlie, the cat's out of the bag. We all now know about the Fencing Cowfish.

Serves 4   **Prep time: 35 minutes, plus marinating time**

Heat rating:

Vegetable oil, for frying
20 won ton skins, cut in half or into triangles
2 tablespoons salt, preferably kosher
1 cup soy sauce
1 cup mirin

2 bunches green onions, white part only, thinly sliced
2 tablespoons toasted sesame seeds
1 pound fresh ahi tuna fillet
1 cup Mango Salsa (page 105)

Heat 1/2 inch of oil in a saucepan over medium-high heat, not allowing it to smoke. Carefully fry the won ton skins in the oil until golden brown on both sides, 10 to 20 seconds. Remove and drain on paper towels. Sprinkle the salt on the won ton chips while they are still warm.

In a large bowl, combine the soy sauce, mirin, green onions, and sesame seeds and stir. Add the ahi, turning to coat. Cover and refrigerate for 1 to 2 hours, turning the fillet in the marinade once or twice while marinating.

Preheat a seasoned cast iron skillet over medium heat without adding any oil to the pan. Remove the ahi fillet from the marinade (reserving marinade), and place directly into the hot skillet. Cook the fillet without moving it, for 6 to 7 minutes on each side for medium doneness. Remove the fillet from the pan and cool slightly. Cut the fillet into a small dice.

Heat the reserved marinade over medium heat until reduced by half. Strain the sauce and reserve.

To serve, arrange the won ton chips on a large serving platter and top with the ahi and Mango Salsa. Spoon some of the sauce over the chips and enjoy.

Rolling in the Onion Patch
Spicy Asian Chicken and Scallion Rolls

This recipe can be a little tricky but is always a hit. The dipping/marinating/basting sauce is good on almost anything. The presentation is definitely a winner.

Serves 12   **Prep time: 1 hour**

Heat rating:

CHICKEN ROLLS
8 small boneless skinless chicken breast halves (about 2 ½ pounds)
8 green onions
1 clove garlic
¼ cup soy sauce
2 tablespoons seasoned rice vinegar
2 teaspoons toasted sesame oil

DIPPING SAUCE
1 red bell pepper, seeded and chopped
¾ cup distilled white vinegar
½ cup sugar
¾ teaspoon crushed red pepper flakes
Salt

⅓ cup mixed black and white sesame seeds
2 to 3 tablespoons vegetable oil

To prepare the chicken rolls, using a mallet, pound each breast until ¾ inch thick between between 2 sheets of plastic wrap. On a cutting board or counter, lay 1 green onion lengthwise on each breast half. Starting from a long side, roll the chicken around the scallion and tie with kitchen string or the outer leaf of a green onion at 1-inch intervals (if this is too difficult pin the roll with a toothpick or two). Trim the green onion flush with chicken. Make 7 more rolls in the same manner.

In a shallow baking dish, stir together the garlic, soy sauce, rice vinegar, and sesame oil. Add the chicken rolls, turning them to coat (the pan should be small enough that the marinade covers most of chicken). Marinate the chicken, covered, in the refrigerator, at least 8 hours and up to 1 day.

To prepare the sauce, purée the bell pepper in a blender with the vinegar. Transfer the mixture to a small saucepan and stir in the sugar, red pepper flakes, and salt to taste. Simmer the sauce 5 minutes, remove from the heat, and cool. (The sauce may be made ahead of time and chilled in an airtight container for up to 3 days.)

Spread the sesame seeds on a sheet of wax paper. Remove the chicken from the marinade, letting the excess drip off, and roll in the sesame seeds to coat. In a large pan, heat 2 tablespoons of the vegetable oil over moderate heat until hot but not smoking, add the rolls in batches, and cook, turning them occasionally, until cooked through, about 10 minutes (add additional vegetable oil if necessary to prevent sticking). It is important that you don't overcook the chicken. Transfer the rolls to a cutting board and cut crosswise into ½-inch-thick slices, discarding the string. Skewer the rolls lengthwise on 6-inch wooden skewers and serve with the dipping sauce.

Piggy Pie
Spicy Pork Empanadas

Call the doctor. I know that you are about to overeat. Try to exert some self-control; much as you'll want to, don't eat all of these by yourself. If you like meat pies, then these will become a staple for you. You can also make mini *empanaditas* or a huge *empanada gallega*.

Serves 6 (about 24 empanadas)   **Prep time: 1 hour, plus 25 minutes baking**

Heat rating:

FILLING
1 tablespoon olive oil
1 (12-ounce) pork tenderloin, trimmed
    and cut into $^1/_3$-inch dice
1 fresh jalapeño chile, stemmed, seeded,
    and minced
2 teaspoons ground chile powder
2 teaspoons ground cumin
$^1/_2$ teaspoon dried chipotle powder
1 $^1/_2$ teaspoons ground cinnamon
1 teaspoon ground allspice
$^1/_2$ cup golden raisins
$^1/_4$ cup freshly squeezed lime juice

6 tablespoons chopped toasted almonds
3 tablespoons sour cream
Pinch of salt
Pinch of freshly ground black pepper

DOUGH
1 $^1/_2$ cups all-purpose flour
1 cup masa harina (corn flour)
1 teaspoon baking powder
1 teaspoon salt
$^1/_2$ cup unsalted butter, melted and cooled
$^1/_2$ cup plus 1 tablespoon water
2 large eggs

To prepare the filling, heat the oil in large, nonstick skillet over medium-high heat. Add the pork, jalapeño, chile powder, cumin, chipotle powder, cinnamon, and allspice to the skillet and cook, stirring, 3 minutes. Add the raisins and lime juice; boil until almost all of the liquid evaporates, about 1 minute. Remove from the heat. Mix in the almonds and sour cream. Season with the salt and pepper. Cool.

To prepare the dough, butter two large baking sheets. Mix the flour, masa harina, baking powder, and salt in a large bowl. Stir in the butter. Whisk the water and 1 of the eggs in a small bowl to blend. Add to the flour mixture. Knead the dough in the bowl until a smooth, pliable dough forms, about 2 minutes. Working with half of the dough at a time, roll out on a floured surface to a $^1/8$-inch thickness. Using a 3 3/4-inch-diameter biscuit cutter, cut out dough into rounds. Reroll the scraps and cut out additional rounds for a total of 12 rounds per dough half.

In a small bowl, whisk the remaining egg. Place 1 tablespoon of filling in the center of each dough round. Lightly brush around the edges with the egg. Fold the dough in half over the filling, pressing the edges with a fork to seal. Place on the prepared baking sheets. (Can be prepared up to this point 1 day ahead. Cover with plastic wrap; chill.)

Preheat the oven to 375°F. Brush the empanadas with the beaten egg. Bake until light golden brown, about 25 minutes.

Acid Fish
Ceviche with Chile Crackers

Ceviche is one of those words that just sounds good. You could rename any mediocre dish ceviche, and I think that it would taste better. Real ceviche is definitely the deal. It is sushi for non–sushi eaters. This version has a little tequila, which is a great twist, but you can omit it if it is a little too high-octane. Since sweet onions have really come into vogue you are going to have to decide for yourself if you want Maui, Vidalia, Walla Walla, or some other variety in your ceviche.

Serves 4 to 6   **Prep time: 20 minutes, plus refrigerator time**

Heat rating:

1 pound fresh seabass, swordfish, red snapper, or halibut fillets

3/4 pound large shrimp, shelled and deveined

1 large sweet onion, peeled and coarsely chopped

3 to 4 small fresh habanero chiles, stemmed, seeded, and finely chopped

1 cup freshly squeezed lime juice

1/2 cup fresh orange juice

6 sprigs cilantro, leaves only, chopped fine

1/2 cup tequila

2 teaspoons salt

1/2 teaspoon ground cayenne pepper

Chile Crackers (recipe follows)

Cilantro leaves, for garnish

Prepare the fillets by removing any bones and remaining skin. Cut into 1 1/2-inch cubes and place in a dish large enough to hold them in one layer. Add the shrimp, onion, and chiles to the fish mixture.

In a separate bowl, combine the citrus juices, cilantro, tequila, salt, and cayenne and mix well. Pour it over the fish mixture. Cover the dish, place it in the refrigerator, and marinate a minimum of 8 hours or until the fish and shrimp are opaque (a light white color on all sides). The acid actually "cooks" the fish, so it is important to check the fish to make sure it is opaque throughout.

Place the ceviche in a serving bowl on a plate surrounded with the Chile Crackers. Garnish with cilantro leaves.

CHILE CRACKERS

Makes 25 to 30 crackers   **Prep time: 1 hour**

Heat rating:

1 ¹/₄ cups all-purpose flour
1 teaspoon kosher salt
¹/₄ teaspoon baking soda
1 teaspoon crushed red pepper flakes,
    ground in a mortar and pestle

¹/₂ teaspoon ground cumin
3 tablespoons canola oil
5 tablespoons plain nonfat yogurt

Preheat the oven to 375°F.

In a large bowl, combine the flour with the salt, baking soda, red pepper flakes, and cumin. Add the oil and yogurt and mix by hand until a firm mass is created, then lightly knead the dough on a flat surface until it becomes smooth. (The dough may be wrapped in plastic and refrigerated at this point until needed, up to 6 hours. Let the dough sit at room temperature to warm slightly before using.)

Divide the dough into 2 equal portions. Working with 1 portion at a time, on a lightly floured work surface, roll the dough out to ¹/8 inch thick. Cut the dough using a 2- to 3-inch cookie cutter, ideally in the shape of a chile. (You may also cut the dough into chile shapes using a sharp knife.) Lightly prick the surface of the cracker with a fork and place on a nonstick (or greased) cookie sheet. Proceed with the remaining dough. Leftover scraps can be recombined, rolled out, and cut.

Bake in the center of the oven for 12 to 15 minutes or until golden brown. Transfer to racks and serve hot or at room temperature. The crackers can be stored in an airtight container for up to 3 days.

Ceviche was actually invented by my great-great-grandmother in 1881 in Wasacj, Poland. She was so poor that she could not afford a stove. Instead she figured she could cook her fish using citrus fruits. Never mind; I made this up.

Searing Soups and Spicy Salads

Jumpin' Jook
Southern Chinese Jook Chile Soup

In China, jook or congee—a porridge of boiled rice and water—is a great base to eat with some sort of meat for breakfast. In San Franciso's Chinatown, the people I know eat it to help with hangovers. While it may be an acquired taste, it is definitely worth a try.

Serves 4 to 6   **Prep time: 2 hours and 15 minutes, plus soaking time**

Heat rating:

2 cups short-grain rice, soaked for
   2 hours in cold water

4 cups water

4 cups chicken stock or broth

SPICY MEATBALLS

1 pound ground lean pork meat

1/4 cup soy sauce

1/4 cup Roasted Chile Oil (recipe follows)

1 tablespoon cornstarch

2 teaspoons salt

1/2 teaspoon freshly ground black pepper

1 to 2 teaspoons crushed red pepper
   flakes

3 green onions, white part only,
   thinly sliced

1 bunch cilantro, stemmed and chopped

4 dried Thai chiles, crushed

6 baby bok choy cabbage, coarsely
   chopped

Fresh cilantro leaves, for garnish

Sliced serrano chiles, for garnish

Drain the rice and combine with the 4 cups water and chicken stock in a large soup pot. Bring to a boil over medium heat, lower the heat, and continue cooking at a simmer until the rice breaks down to a creamy consistency, 1 1/2 to 2 hours. If needed, add more chicken stock to keep a smooth, moist consistency.

While the rice is cooking, prepare the spicy meatballs by combining all of the meatball ingredients in a mixing bowl and stirring with a spoon or mixing by hand until smooth and uniformly combined. Shape into meatballs 1 inch in diameter and place on a baking sheet. Refrigerate until the rice porridge is almost finished.

Add the green onions, cilantro, chiles, and bok choy to the rice mixture.

Fifteen minutes prior to serving, place the meatballs into the soup and allow them to cook through so that no pink remains in the center of the meatballs. Ladle the soup into serving bowls and garnish with the cilantro leaves and serrano chiles.

ROASTED CHILE OIL

Makes 1 cup **Prep time: 20 minutes**

Heat rating:

10 dried chiles de árbol or dried Thai
   chiles, stems removed
1 cup canola oil

 Get everyone out of the kitchen, and open a window—the smoke you will create won't be appreciated by the nonchilehead.

Preheat your oven broiler. Place the chiles under the broiler in a pan for 1 to 2 minutes, shaking occasionally, until they start to release their fragrance. Remove from the broiler, and try to steer clear of the smoke! Grind up the chiles in a mortar and pestle or process in a food processor until coarsely ground. Transfer to a bowl and set aside.

Place the oil in a pan and slowly warm to a moderate heat, about 4 minutes. Remove the oil from the heat and pour over the chiles. Steep until room temperature and strain into a glass jar. Cover and refrigerate until ready to use. The chile oil should keep its strong flavor for a week or so.

Legend has it that the Incas burned chiles to create a wall of smoke to ward off Spanish invaders. Apparently the smoke irritated the Spaniards' eyes and drove them away.

Uncle Pablo's Famous Chile Soup
Ajo Chile Soup with Grilled Nopales and Corn

If you want to enjoy a delicious dish, try this recipe. If you want to show how tough you are, try this recipe with the thorns on the nopales and add six habaneros. Just kidding about the thorns bit; those things have got to go, no matter how macho you think you are! Fresh and canned nopales can be found in Latin markets.

Serves 6   Prep time: 1 hour

Heat rating:

1 pound fresh nopales (cactus ears), or 1 (12-ounce) can prepared nopalito strips, drained

Vegetable oil, for coating

2 dried ajo chiles or other mild, dried chiles

8 cups chicken stock or broth

3 cloves garlic, finely minced

1 ear corn, husked and cut into 1/2-inch wheels

1/2 bunch cilantro, stemmed and coarsely chopped

2 shallots, finely minced

Juice of 1 lime

Salt and freshly ground black pepper

Fresh cilantro leaves, for garnish

Lime wedges, for garnish

Warm tortillas, for serving

Prepare a fire in a charcoal grill or preheat a gas grill to medium-high heat.

Clean the nopales with a vegetable peeler (you may want to wear kitchen gloves), removing any remaining thorns (watch your knuckles). Lightly oil the surface of the nopales with vegetable oil and place them on the grill or under the broiler, turning every 3 to 4 minutes. The cactus should be softened and dark brown in color. Coarsely chop. (If using canned nopalitos, drain them thoroughly, coarsely chop, and set aside.)

In a small bowl, cover the chiles with boiling water and allow to steep for a minimum of 5 minutes. Drain the chiles and stem, seed, and coarsely chop them. Combine with the chicken stock, chopped nopales, garlic, corn, cilantro, and shallots in a soup pot over medium heat. Bring to a simmer and cook until the corn is cooked and the nopales are soft, 12 to 15 minutes.

Add the lime juice and season with salt and pepper to taste. Ladle the soup into serving bowls and garnish with the cilantro leaves and lime wedges. Serve with warm tortillas.

Crabby Aunt Shu Lin's Soup

Thai Crab and Baby Corn Soup

Crabby or not, you'll love this soup. If you don't, then you probably just need an attitude adjustment.

Serves 6   **Prep time: 50 minutes**

Heat rating:

8 cups chicken or shrimp broth

2 stalks lemongrass, thinly sliced crosswise into little discs about 6 inches up from the base

1 bay leaf

1 tablespoon finely minced fresh cilantro

1/4 cup kaffir lime leaves (available in Asian markets; optional)

2 (15-ounce) cans baby corn, rinsed and well drained

1 1/2 pounds fresh or frozen crabmeat

Juice of 1 lime

3 fresh red Thai chiles, stemmed, seeded, and very finely minced

2 green onions, white part only, very thinly sliced

2 teaspoons salt

1 teaspoon ground white pepper

6 sprigs basil, for garnish

1/2 lime, sliced, for garnish

In a large soup pot or stockpot over medium-high heat, combine the broth, lemongrass, bay leaf, cilantro, and lime leaves and bring to a simmer. Continue to simmer, covered, until the lemongrass and lime leaves are softened, about 15 minutes.

Remove the lime leaves and add the corn, crabmeat, lime juice, chiles, green onions, salt, and pepper, stirring to incorporate. Reduce the heat to very low and cover. Continue to cook the soup over very low heat until all ingredients are tender and the soup is heated through, approximately 15 minutes.

To serve, ladle the soup into preheated soup bowls, giving each serving a good amount of the crab, corn, and chiles. Garnish with a sprig of basil and a slice of lime.

Until you build up a resistance to the oils in chiles, you should use latex or kitchen gloves when working with them. It sounds silly, but you only have to rub your eyes once, even if you think you've washed your hands, and you'll never work with chiles without gloves again.

A Thriller in Manila
Manila Clams in Red Chile Broth

It doesn't taste like a butterfly, but it stings like a bee. Don't get me wrong, I have never actually eaten a butterfly. If I were to eat one, I guess deep-fried would be the way to go. Anyway, this recipe is really easy and tasty. It is great for dinner parties or special occasions. This can also be made with 1/4 cup white wine and 1 tablespoon of butter in the broth.

Serves 4   **Prep time: 25 minutes**

Heat rating:

4 cloves garlic
6 Roma (plum) tomatoes
48 baby Manila, littleneck, cherrystone, or small steamer clams
4 tablespoons extra virgin olive oil

1 cup water
1 cup clam broth or bottled clam juice
1/2 teaspoon Hurtin' Habanero Hot Sauce or other Louisiana-style hot sauce

Preheat the oven to 450°F. Place the garlic and tomatoes on a baking sheet in the center of the oven and roast, 30 to 40 minutes, until the garlic is tender and the tomatoes are charred. Remove from the oven, let cool slightly, then chop coarsely.

Scrub the clams and set aside. In a saucepan, heat 1 tablespoon of the olive oil over medium heat. Add the garlic, tomatoes, clams, 1/2 cup of the water, and 1/2 cup of the broth. Cover and let steam until the clams open, about 3 minutes. Discard any clams that do not open.

Using a slotted spoon or tongs, carefully transfer the clams to individual serving bowls, dividing equally. Add the remaining 1/2 cup of water, 1/2 cup of broth, 3 table-spoons of olive oil, and the hot sauce to the saucepan and cook for 2 minutes more, until heated through. Ladle the broth into the serving bowls, dividing equally, and serve immediately.

Screamin' Steamin' Seafood
Spicy Seafood Stew

A lot of alliteration makes a marvelous meal.

Serves 8   **Prep time: 1 hour and 15 minutes**

Heat rating: 🌶 🌶 🌶 🌶 🌶 (with Insanity Sauce)

2 tablespoons butter
2 tablespoons olive oil
1 cup chopped onion
1/2 cup chopped celery
1 clove garlic, minced
1/4 cup all-purpose flour
4 cups fish stock or clam juice
2 cups shucked oysters, liquid reserved
1 (12-ounce) can tomatoes
1/2 cup dry white wine
1 tablespoon freshly squeezed
    lemon juice

2 tablespoons chopped fresh parsley
1 bay leaf
1/2 teaspoon salt
1/2 teaspoon Cool Cayenne Pepper Sauce
    or Louisiana-style hot sauce
3 drops Insanity Sauce (optional)
1/2 teaspoon powdered saffron
2 pounds fish fillets, such as halibut,
    cut in 1 1/2-inch chunks
8 ounces shrimp, peeled and deveined
1 cup fresh crabmeat
Steamed rice, for serving

🌶 In a large pot over medium-high heat, melt the butter with the olive oil. Add the onion, celery, and garlic and sauté until the vegetables are tender, about 7 minutes. Sprinkle with the flour. Stir and cook until light brown, about 5 minutes. Slowly stir in the fish stock along with the reserved oyster liquid.

Add the tomatoes, wine, lemon juice, parsley, bay leaf, salt, Cool Cayenne Pepper Sauce, Insanity Sauce, and saffron. Simmer on low heat, covered, for 1 hour. Add the fish and cook for 10 minutes. Add the shrimp, oysters, and crab meat and cook 5 more minutes, until the shrimp are opaque. Serve over rice.

Rinse all fish prior to cooking and check to make sure all the bones and skin have been removed. Bones can be removed from most fish using clean needle-nose pliers. After rinsing, pat the fillets dry using a paper or cloth towel prior to use with any of these recipes.

Searing Skirt Salad
Grilled Lemongrass Beef and Noodle Salad

This is a great recipe, but you may wonder which meat option to choose. At my restaurant we always found the fattier skirt steak to be more tender and to work better with our marinades. Some people prefer the flavor of flank steak, but either meat will be delicious in this dish. Just pick out a good pair of chopsticks and enjoy the flavor of Asia. You should be able to find the ingredients for this recipe in Asian markets and many well-stocked supermarkets.

Serves 4   Prep time: 35 minutes, plus marinating time

Heat rating:

MARINADE

2 stalks fresh lemongrass, outer leaves discarded and root end trimmed

6 cloves garlic, coarsley chopped

1-inch piece fresh gingerroot, peeled

2 tablespoons nuoc nam (fish sauce)

1 tablespoon soy sauce

4 teaspoons sugar

2 tablespoons vegetable oil

1/2 teaspoon toasted sesame oil

1/4 teaspoon sherry

1 to 1 1/4 pounds beef skirt steak or flank steak

8 ounces dried rice-stick noodles (rice vermicelli)

1 cup nuoc cham (seasoned fish sauce)

1 pound seedless (European) cucumber, halved lengthwise and cut diagonally into 1/4-inch-thick slices

1/2 cup loosely packed fresh basil leaves (preferably Thai basil)

1/2 cup loosely packed fresh mint leaves

1/2 cup loosely packed fresh cilantro leaves

2 tablespoons toasted rice powder

2 to 4 small thin fresh Thai or serrano chiles, seeded and sliced very thin

To prepare the marinade, make thin slices across the bottom 6 inches of the lemongrass (you will have little discs). Throw away the top part of the stalks. In a food processor, mince the lemongrass, garlic, and ginger. Add the nuoc nam, soy sauce, sugar, oils, and sherry and pulse a few times to blend.

Place the meat and marinade into a large, resealable plastic bag. Marinate the steak in the refrigerator for 6 to 8 hours turning the bag over every so often to distribute the marinade. (This is a great way to marinate anything without a mess.)

To prepare the noodles, cover them with hot water and soak until they are barely softened (for about 15 minutes).

Prepare a fire in a charcoal grill or preheat a gas grill to high heat. Bring enough salted water for the noodles to a boil in a large pot. Cook the steak on the grill for about 5 minutes on each side, or until it is cooked the way you like it. Let the meat stand for 5 minutes (this allows the juices in the meat to redistribute and not end up on the cutting board). Slice the steak across the grain on a diagonal and set aside.

Drain the soaked noodles and put them into the pot of boiling water for about 1 minute, or until soft. Drain the noodles and rinse them under cold water so they stop cooking.

In a bowl, toss the noodles with the nuoc cham. Transfer to a serving platter and arrange the sliced steak on top. Top with the cucumber, herbs, toasted rice powder, and chiles and serve.

You might want to remove the skin of any chile you are not going to mince or grind up; the skin is really hard to digest. It comes off easily if you roast the whole chiles over a fire until they blister, then put them in a bowl and cover it tightly with plastic wrap, and let it sit for a few minutes. The steam will pull the skin away from the flesh and you can remove it with your hands without losing much flavor. If you ever see someone getting the roasted skin off by scrubbing it under running water, politely get up and leave. Don't ever go back to their house for dinner again. They have just washed away the poor chile's flavor.

Cuook Yum Ooh
Chinese Cucumber Salad

Quick, easy, and tasty is what this dish is. It is a great accompaniment to chicken satay or chicken curries.

Serves 6   Prep time: 30 minutes, plus 2 hours marinating time

Heat rating:

3 cucumbers
1 teaspoon salt
3 tablespoons Soyabi Sauce or soy sauce
1 cup rice wine vinegar
1 tablespoon sugar

1 teaspoon toasted sesame oil
2 tablespoons finely chopped green onion, white part only
1/4 teaspoon Garlic-Chile Sauce or Asian garlic-chile paste

Peel the cucumbers and slice thinly crosswise. Place in a large bowl. In a small bowl, mix the remaining ingredients and pour over the cucumbers. Stir carefully. Cover and refrigerate for 2 hours before serving.

Them Shrimp Are Fruity
Spicy Grilled Shrimp and Melon Salad

Have your shrimp been acting strange lately? Don't worry; a little marinade and melon will put them back where you want them. The secret to making this salad is to cool the grilled shrimp in their shells at room temperature rather than refrigerating them, which can toughen and dry them out, and to peel them at the last minute. Feel free to use any combination of melons: only the watermelon is a must!

Serves 4   **Prep time: 30 minutes, plus 2 hours marinating time**

Heat rating:

MARINADE
1 pinch Insanity Spice or dried habanero powder
1 1/2 cups olive oil
1 teaspoon salt
2 cloves garlic, sliced
1 bunch cilantro, stemmed and chopped
2 tablespoons freshly squeezed lime juice

32 to 36 medium shrimp, heads removed (about 1 1/2 pounds)

4 cups 1/2-inch melon cubes (such as watermelon, cantaloupe, and honeydew)
3 tablespoons sugar
1/2 cup firmly packed fresh mint leaves, finely chopped
2 tablespoons freshly squeezed lime juice
1 tablespoon rice wine vinegar
Leaves of 1 head romaine lettuce, ribs removed and cut in wide strips

To prepare the marinade, in a large bowl, mix the Insanity Spice, oil, salt, garlic, cilantro, and lime juice. Reserve about 1/4 cup of the marinade for the salad. Add the shrimp to the remaining marinade and marinate for 2 to 3 hours in the refrigerator.

In a bowl, combine the melon, sugar, mint, lime juice, and vinegar and refrigerate for at least 30 minutes and up to 2 hours.

Prepare a fire in a charcoal grill or preheat a gas grill to high heat. Remove the shrimp from the marinade. Grill the shrimp for about 3 minutes, turning once, until opaque. Set aside to cool. Toss the romaine with the 1/4 cup reserved marinade, and form a bed of the greens on individual serving plates. Drain the melons slightly and place over the romaine on each plate. Peel the shrimp and arrange over the melon, dividing equally. Serve immediately.

And the Cow Jumped into the Salad
Western Steak Salad

Uncle Roy used to rustle up this dish while driving the herd. Pull up a campfire, grab your bedroll, and dig in. Just don't sit on your heels, if wearing spurs.

Serves 4   **Prep time: 45 minutes, plus overnight refrigeration**

Heat rating:

1 cup unsalted beef broth
3 dried ancho chiles
4 large cloves garlic
1 1/2 teaspoons ground cumin
1 pound beef flank steak, well trimmed
Salt
2 onions, sliced
2 fresh Anaheim chiles, quartered, seeded, and thinly sliced crosswise
1 red bell pepper, quartered, seeded, and thinly sliced

1 large head romaine lettuce, thinly sliced (6 to 8 cups)
2 cups fresh or drained canned corn
2 large tomatoes, chopped
1/2 cup loosely packed fresh cilantro leaves
1 teaspoon distilled white vinegar
1 cup grated mozzarella cheese
1/4 cup crumbled tortilla chips

In a saucepan over high heat, boil the broth and the ancho chiles for 4 minutes. Remove from the heat, cover, and let stand for about 20 minutes, or until soft. Drain the chiles, reserving the liquid. Rinse, stem, and seed the chiles. Put the soaked chiles, garlic, and cumin in a blender and purée until smooth. Remove 1/3 cup of the purée and set aside. Spread the remaining purée over both sides of the beef and season with salt. Place the beef in a large, resealable plastic bag and refrigerate overnight.

In a medium pan, simmer the reserved steeping liquid, onions, Anaheim chiles, and bell pepper until tender, about 5 minutes. Cool and set aside.

Prepare a fire in charcoal grill, preheat a gas grill to medium-high heat, or pre-heat the broiler. Cook the beef for about 5 minutes per side or to desired doneness. Remove the beef and let it rest for about 10 minutes before slicing across the grain into 1/4-inch-thick slices. If you cook the beef in the broiler, the pan will have some tasty juices that will fortify your reserved purée. If not, don't sweat it.

To serve, place the lettuce, corn, tomatoes, and cilantro in a large serving bowl. Sprinkle the vinegar over the lettuce and toss gently. Top with the cheese, tortilla chips, onion mixture, and beef strips. Serve with the reserved purée on the side.

"Ancho" is Spanish for "broad," an accurate description of this dried chile's fresh counterpart, the poblano. This plump, rounded chile is very commonly used dried, and you can taste why. To kick up the flavor a notch add a little dried chile de árbol.

Tortuous Thai Noodle Salad
Thai Peanut–Pasta Salad

There is nothing a like a refreshing cool salad with a clean burn. This is especially true when combined with a delicious peanut sauce and one of many great Asian noodles. If you have never experimented with pasta from Thailand, Japan, or China, there is no time like the present. Since ba-mee noodles are not a neighborhood market staple, you can substitute dried soba noodles or rice noodles, which are widely available.

Serves 4 to 6   **Prep time: 25 minutes**

Heat rating:

8 ounces dried Thai ba-mee noodles (wheat egg noodles)
2 teaspoons peanut oil
1 teaspoon toasted sesame oil
2 teaspoons soy sauce
4 ounces snow peas, sliced diagonally

THAI PEANUT DRESSING
2 cloves garlic
1 cup creamy peanut butter
3 tablespoons sugar
1/2 cup water
1/2 teaspoon Garlic-Chile Sauce or Asian garlic-chile paste

Juice of 1 lemon
2 tablespoons soy sauce
1 teaspoon salt
1/2 teaspoon freshly ground black pepper

1 red bell pepper, roasted, peeled, stemmed, seeded, and cut into thin strips
3 fresh Thai chiles, stemmed, seeded, and coarsely chopped
3 green onions, thinly sliced and white part separated from green part

Cook the ba-mee noodles in a large pot of boiling water until al dente. Drain and rinse. Toss the ba-mee noodles with the oils and soy sauce in a large bowl and set aside to cool. Blanch the snow peas in a pan of boiling water for 2 minutes. Drain and cool rapidly in a bowl of ice water to stop the cooking process. Drain and reserve.

To prepare the dressing, place the garlic, peanut butter, sugar, water, Garlic-Chile Sauce, lemon juice, soy sauce, salt, and pepper in a food processor and pulse until smooth. Add more water, by the tablespoonful, until a ketchuplike consistency is reached. Adjust the seasonings to taste.

Combine the noodles, snow peas, bell pepper, chiles, and the white parts of the green onions. Toss with two-thirds of the dressing, cover, and refrigerate until cool, for at least 15 minutes and up to 3 hours. Cover the remaining one-third dressing and refrigerate as well.

To serve, arrange a mound of noodle salad in the center of a serving plate so that a few snow peas from the salad are on top. Drizzle the remaining dressing over the top. Garnish with the green parts of the green onions and serve.

A Cowboy Named Julius
Southwestern Caesar Salad with Chipotle Dressing

Hail Caesar—Cardini that is. His 1924 invention of the Caesar salad has deeply affected my life, or at least my mealtimes. This variation may sound strange, but it tastes wonderful.

Serves 4   Prep time: 15 minutes

Heat rating: **(with Insanity Sauce)**

DRESSING
1/2 cup mayonnaise
1 1/2 tablespoons water
1 tablespoon soy sauce
1 tablespoon freshly squeezed lemon juice
1/2 tablespoon freshly grated lemon zest
1 tablespoon minced drained canned chipotle chiles in adobo sauce
1 fresh red jalapeño, stemmed, seeded, and minced
1 to 2 drops Insanity Sauce (optional)

1 teaspoon firmly packed light brown sugar
Salt
Freshly ground black pepper

1 large head romaine lettuce, torn into bite-size pieces
2 medium tomatoes, diced
1/2 cup fresh or drained canned corn kernels
1/4 cup freshly grated Parmesan cheese

To prepare the dressing, in a small bowl mix together the mayonnaise, water, soy sauce, lemon juice and zest, chiles, Insanity Sauce, and brown sugar. Season the dressing to taste with salt and pepper and set aside.

Toss together the romaine, tomatoes, corn, 2 tablespoons of the cheese, and the salad dressing. Sprinkle the remaining cheese on the tossed salad and serve.

Fresh chiles have lots of vitamins A and C and are a pretty good source of vitamin E, potassium, and folic acid. They retain their vitamin C if frozen or canned, but lose it if they are dried. Fresh chiles are also very low in sodium, and because they are vegetables, they have no cholesterol. Red chiles have more vitamin A than green chiles.

Shanghai Straw
Asian Slaw

Tired of the same old coleslaw? You need Shanghai Straw, a slaw with Asian ingredients that is both healthier and, might I say, tastier than traditional coleslaw. Napa cabbage is a milder cousin of the green cabbage. One of the great aspects of this recipe is that you can eat the roasted peanuts while you cook.

Serves 4   **Prep time: 20 minutes**

Heat rating:

DRESSING
3/8 cup vegetable oil
1/4 cup rice vinegar
2 1/2 tablespoons peeled minced fresh gingerroot
1 tablespoon soy sauce
1 tablespoon freshly squeezed lemon juice
Pinch of ground cayenne pepper

6 cups thinly sliced napa cabbage (about 1 large cabbage)
6 green onions, white part only, very thinly sliced
6 ounces snow peas, stringed and thinly sliced lengthwise
1 small yellow bell pepper, seeded and thinly sliced
1 small red bell pepper, seeded and thinly sliced
1/2 cup roasted peanuts
Salt and freshly ground black pepper

To prepare the dressing, whisk all of the dressing ingredients in a bowl to blend. Mix the cabbage, green onions, snow peas, bell pepper, and peanuts in a large bowl. Toss with enough of the dressing to coat. Season with salt and pepper to taste. (Can be made 3 hours ahead; cover and chill.)

Scorching Sides

Spuds and Suds
Beer-Roasted New Potatoes   49

Eye-Popping Corn Cakes
Green Onion Corn Cakes   50

Arroz con Spicy
Spicy Spanish Rice   51

Chillin' Chile Cornbread
Cornbread with Green Chiles   52

Virulent Veggies
Escabèche   53

Once Broiled, Twice Shy
Oven-Broiled Stuffed Potatoes with
Chiles and Cheddar Cheese   54

Smoke Rings
Chipotle Fried Onion Rings   55

Pop-Eye's Potato Snacks
Spicy Spinach Samosas   56

Electric Eggplant
Spicy Chinese Eggplant   57

Dr. Mojo's Plastic Surgery Potatoes
Brined Potatoes with
Mojo Sauce   58

Roly Poly Escarole
Sautéed Escarole   59

Barking Puppies
Hush Puppies   60

Rabid Rabe
Spicy Broccoli Rabe   61

Louisiana Love
Spicy Red Beans and Rice   62

Popcorn Puddin'
Cheesy Polenta with Green Chiles   63

Spears and Seeds
Sesame Asparagus   64

Penang Pasta

Spicy Pasta—Asian Style   65

Arroza Sabrosa

Tex-Mex Rice   66

Frito's Rice

Sofrito Rice   67

Sugar and Spice

Whipped Chipotle Sweet
Potatoes   68

No Stuffed Shirts

Chile Cornbread Stuffing I   69

Pining and Combining

Chile Cornbread Stuffing II   70

Grit It Out

Roasted Pepper Grits   71

Mr. Toad's Spicy Ride

Roasted Mushrooms with
Tomatillo Salsa   72

Spuds and Suds
Beer-Roasted New Potatoes

The fun of this dish is figuring out which beer to use. How about a lambic or a bock beer? Too intense? Try a nice wheat beer such as hefeweizen. Big game on TV and can't get to the store? Then grab a Bud for your spud. I personally recommend using a dark beer, because of its darker flavor. Serve with any beef or pork dish.

Serves 4   **Prep time: 1 hour and 20 minutes**

Heat rating:

6 fresh Anaheim chiles
2 pounds red potatoes, cut into large chunks
1 yellow onion, coarsely chopped
1 tablespoon ground cumin

1 tablespoon salt
$^1/_2$ teaspoon freshly ground black pepper
1 teaspoon ground cayenne pepper
3 cloves garlic, finely minced
3 cups beer

Preheat the oven to 450°F.

Roast the chiles under a broiler or over a grill or gas burner, until charred. Enclose the chiles in a paper bag or place in a bowl and cover with plastic wrap. Let stand for 5 to 10 minutes, until the skins begin to peel away. Peel, seed, and chop the chiles.

Combine the potatoes, onion, and chiles in a large, ovenproof baking dish. Combine the cumin, salt, pepper, garlic, and beer in a separate bowl and pour over the potato mixture.

Place the potatoes in the center of the oven and bake, uncovered, for 15 minutes. Reduce the temperature to 300°F and continue cooking for an additional 30 to 45 minutes longer, or until the potatoes are golden brown and soft. Remove from the oven and cool slightly before serving.

Eye-Popping Corn Cakes
Green Onion Corn Cakes

These corn cakes are really easy to make and very tasty. Serve as a side dish with chicken or shellfish. You can also make mini cakes and serve them as an appetizer.

Serves 4   Prep time: 30 minutes

Heat rating:

3/4 cup all-purpose flour
1/2 cup quick-cooking polenta or finely ground cornmeal
1/2 teaspoon baking powder
1/2 teaspoon baking soda
1 teaspoon salt
1 teaspoon sugar
1 cup fresh corn kernels

3 1/4 cups buttermilk, plus additional as needed
2 tablespoons butter, melted
1 egg, beaten
2 green onions, white part only, chopped
1/4 cup Garlic-Chile Sauce or Asian garlic-chile paste
1 teaspoon vegetable oil

In a bowl, combine the flour, polenta, baking powder, baking soda, salt, and sugar and mix well. In a food processor, purée 1/2 cup of the corn with 2 cups of the buttermilk. In a large bowl, whisk together the butter and remaining 1 1/4 cups of buttermilk. Add the egg and the corn purée and stir well. Add the flour mixture and stir to combine. Stir in the remaining 1/2 cup corn, green onions, and Garlic-Chile Sauce. Thin with additional buttermilk if necessary.

In a sauté pan over medium heat, heat the oil. Ladle 1/2 cup of the batter into the pan, one layer at a time. Cook until just golden brown, about 8 minutes. Flip and repeat. Transfer to a paper towel–lined baking sheet to drain. Repeat for the remaining corn cakes.

Arroz con Spicy
Spicy Spanish Rice

Good solid rice dishes like this one really round out a meal. Nothing fancy, just delicious.

Serves 6   **Prep time: 40 minutes**

Heat rating:

¹/₂ green bell pepper, seeded and chopped	1 cup long-grain white rice
¹/₂ red bell pepper, seeded and chopped	2 cups water
1 medium onion, thinly sliced	1 large tomato, peeled and chopped
1 clove garlic, minced	¹/₂ teaspoon salt
2 tablespoons olive oil	¹/₂ teaspoon freshly ground black pepper
¹/₂ teaspoon dried basil	¹/₂ teaspoon Cool Cayenne Pepper Sauce or other Louisiana-style hot sauce
¹/₂ teaspoon fresh rosemary leaves, chopped	

In a large skillet, sauté the bell peppers, onion, and garlic in the olive oil until tender. Stir in the basil, rosemary, rice, water, tomato, salt, pepper, and Cool Cayenne Pepper Sauce. Bring to a boil over moderately high heat. Cover, turn heat to low, and cook for about 20 minutes or until the rice is tender and the liquid is absorbed.

Chile peppers are not related to black pepper at all. After encountering chiles, Columbus thought he had discovered a new kind of pepper, and we've been stuck with the name ever since.

Chillin' Chile Cornbread
Cornbread with Green Chiles

To make this right, get out your butter churner. Churn till your arms feel like they will fall off. Drain off the milk still in the churn and you will get richer, creamier bread. Actually, dairies now use bacteria to make buttermilk, so you can burn that churn and go get some physical therapy. They should pass a law requiring all restaurants to serve cornbread. I love it. Try this recipe and you will too. In fact, they should pass a law requiring you to try it.

Serves 8   **Prep time: 45 minutes**

Heat rating:

2 fresh green New Mexico chiles
2 cups coarsely ground yellow cornmeal
2 1/2 cups all-purpose flour
3 tablespoons sugar
1/2 teaspoon salt
2 teaspoons baking powder

2 large eggs, lightly beaten
1 cup buttermilk
1 cup milk
6 tablespoons butter, melted
1 cup shredded Monterey Jack

Roast the chiles under a broiler or over a grill or gas burner, until charred. Enclose the chiles in a paper bag or place in a bowl and cover with plastic wrap. Let stand for 5 to 10 minutes, until the skins begin to peel away. Peel, seed, and chop the chiles and set aside.

Preheat the oven to 400°F. While preheating, place a 9 by 13-inch baking pan in the oven to warm.

In a mixing bowl, combine the cornmeal, flour, sugar, salt, and baking powder. In a separate bowl combine eggs, buttermilk, milk, butter, cheese, and roasted chiles; mix to blend. Fold the egg mixture into the dry ingredients just until moist. Butter the preheated pan and immediately pour in the batter. Bake for 25 minutes, or until the cornbread is brown around the edges and the top is firm. This recipe can also be used to make mini muffins for appetizers.

Be sure to use fresh eggs! As we say around Dave's kitchen, "When in doubt, throw it out!" Even though most commercial raw egg products are pasteurized, be extra careful when using anything like mayonnaise or tartar sauce. Keep time out of refrigeration to a minimum for these items, and for recipes containing them.

Virulent Veggies
Escabèche

This dish is to chileheads what stretching and warming up is to athletes. Eating this won't guarantee you'll avoid pulling a muscle during dinner. It will, however, make sure that you stay warm between dishes.

Serves plenty (makes about 6 cups)

Prep time: 25 minutes, plus marinating time

Heat rating:

1 teaspoon vegetable oil
1/2 cup distilled white vinegar
Juice of 1 lime
2 teaspoons ground cumin
1/4 teaspoon salt
1/4 teaspoon freshly ground black pepper
3 large carrots, sliced (about 1 cup) and cooked al dente

1 small yellow or red onion, sliced into long, thin strips
1 cup small radishes, whole
2 cups drained canned pickled jalapeño or caribe chiles (mixed whole and sliced) plus 1 cup reserved pickling liquid

 In a blender or food processor, combine the oil, vinegar, lime juice, cumin, salt, and pepper and blend for 1 minute.

Place the vegetables, chiles, and vinaigrette in a large bowl and mix together until the vegetables are well coated. Add reserved chile pickling juice to taste. Cover and refrigerate for at least 2 hours or overnight.

Called "escovitch" in Jamaica and "escebèche" in France and Spain, this spicy marinade is typically meant for fish. Who has time to go fishing though? I like it as a snack.

Once Broiled, Twice Shy

Oven-Broiled Stuffed Potatoes with Chiles and Cheddar Cheese

This is a fancy way of making twice-baked potatoes. Trust me, it is worth the effort. You might even want to add some bacon bits and/or chives.

Serves 4   **Prep time: 1 hour**

Heat rating: (with Insanity Sauce)

4 medium baking potatoes (about 10 ounces each), halved lengthwise

2 tablespoons vegetable oil

1 cup chopped yellow onion

1/2 cup chopped celery

1/2 cup chopped seeded green bell pepper or poblano chile

2 cloves garlic, minced finely

1 (16-ounce) can tomatoes, drained and chopped

2 drops Insanity Sauce (optional)

1 teaspoon dried oregano, crushed

1 teaspoon dried thyme, crushed

2 teaspoons salt

1/2 teaspoon freshly ground black pepper

1 cup grated Cheddar cheese

Preheat the oven to 350°F and lightly oil an ovenproof baking pan. Place the potatoes, cut side down, in the pan and roast until tender but still firm, 35 to 45 minutes. Remove from the oven and cool slightly. Scoop the flesh from the inside of the potato halves into a bowl, reserving the shells intact. Mash the reserved potato pulp lightly and set aside to cool.

Heat the oil in a sauté pan over medium-high heat, but do not allow it to smoke. Sauté the onion, celery, bell peppers, and garlic until softened but not browned, 5 to 6 minutes. Add the tomatoes, Insanity Sauce, oregano, thyme, salt, and pepper to the pan and cook until all of the excess liquid has evaporated. Add the reserved potato pulp and the cheese, stirring to incorporate. Remove from the heat and let cool slightly.

Stuff the mixture back into the potato shells, dividing equally, and place the shells stuffed sides up in an ovenproof baking dish or pan. Return to the oven and bake for an additional 10 to 15 minutes, or until the crust is set and lightly golden brown.

Smoke Rings
Chipotle Fried Onion Rings

These are a chilehead twist on a great American dish. They seem to just go up in smoke and, if you add Insanity Spice, you will too. Use your leftover chipotle rub next time you bake chicken, fish, or pork chops. Look for the chipotle and ancho chile powders at Latin or gourmet markets.

Serves 4   **Prep time: 30 minutes**

Heat rating:  **(with Insanity Spice)**

CHIPOTLE RUB
3/4 teaspoon oregano powder
3 tablespoons dried chipotle powder
1/4 cup ancho chile powder
3 tablespoons granulated garlic
1 cup coarse salt

1/2 teaspoon Insanity Spice (optional)

2 white onions
Corn oil, for deep-frying
1/2 cup all-purpose flour

To make the Chipotle Rub, in a small heavy skillet mix the oregano, chipotle and chile powders, garlic, salt, and Insanity Spice and dry-roast over moderate heat, shaking the skillet occasionally, until fragrant and beginning to brown, about 2 minutes. Remove from the heat and cool.

To make the onion rings, preheat the oven to 250°F and line a large baking sheet with paper towels. Slice the onion and separate into rings. In a deep pot or deep-fryer heat 2 inches of oil to 375°F.

While the oil is heating, in a large bowl stir together the flour and 2 teaspoons of the Chipotle Rub. (Store the remaining Chipotle Rub in an airtight container; do not refrigerate.) Add the onion rings and toss well to coat. Transfer the onion rings to a large sieve and shake gently to remove excess flour mixture.

Add a handful of onion rings to the hot oil and fry, stirring with tongs, until crisp and golden brown, about 30 seconds. Transfer with a slotted spoon to the paper towel–lined baking sheet to drain. Fry the remaining onion rings in the same manner. (The onion rings may be made 15 minutes ahead of serving and kept warm in a 250°F oven.)

Popeye's Potato Snacks
Spicy Spinach Samosas

Popeye can keep his canned spinach. I'll take these instead. If you have never had samosas—savory filled pastries from India—then this recipe will be a treat.

Serves 8 (about 25 samosas)   **Prep time: 40 minutes**

Heat rating:

FILLING
8 ounces red potatoes
1 tablespoon fennel seeds
1 tablespoon ground cumin
$1/2$ teaspoon turmeric
$1/4$ cup vegetable oil
1 onion, chopped
3 small fresh serrano or Thai chiles,
    seeded and minced
1 (2-inch) piece fresh gingerroot, peeled
    and finely grated

3 cloves garlic, minced
1 pound fresh spinach (3 cups packed),
    stemmed
Salt and freshly ground black pepper

10 (17 by 12-inch) phyllo sheets, thawed
    if frozen, stacked between 2 sheets
    wax paper, and covered with a
    kitchen towel
$1/2$ cup unsalted butter, melted
Fresh mint leaves, for garnish
Mango chutney, for serving

To prepare the filling, in a saucepan simmer the potatoes in salted water to cover until barely tender, about 12 minutes. Drain. Cut the potatoes into $1/4$-inch dice.

In a heavy skillet, dry-roast the fennel seeds, cumin, and turmeric over moderate heat, stirring occasionally, until fragrant and several shades darker, about 2 minutes (be careful not to burn them, as it can happen quickly). Add the oil, onion, chiles, ginger, and garlic and cook, stirring, until the onion is softened. Add the potatoes and spinach and sauté over moderately high heat, stirring, until the spinach is wilted but still bright green, about 2 minutes. Season the filling with salt and pepper to taste and cool. (The filling may be made 1 day ahead and chilled, covered.)

Preheat the oven to 400°F and lightly grease a baking sheet.

On a flat work surface, arrange 1 phyllo sheet with a long side facing you and, using a pastry brush, brush lightly with some of the melted butter. Top with a second phyllo sheet and brush it lightly with butter. Cut stacked phyllo lengthwise into 5 strips, each 12 by about 3 $1/2$ inches. Put 2 heaping tablespoons of filling near the top corner of each strip and fold the corner of phyllo opposite the filling down and over to enclose filling, forming a triangle. Continue folding the strip down, maintaining a triangle shape. Put the samosa, seam side down, on baking sheet and cover with plastic wrap. Make 24 more samosas with the remaining phyllo and filling in the same manner. (The samosas may be prepared up to this point up to 6 hours ahead and chilled, covered.) Bake the samosas in the center of the oven until golden brown, about 10 minutes. Transfer to a serving platter. Garnish with mint and serve warm with chutney on the side.

Electric Eggplant
Spicy Chinese Eggplant

Eggplant is a flavor sponge. In this recipe it soaks up great Asian tastes and then lends its own fresh buttery flavor. With its fiery chile bite, this dish is like Chinese New Year— a happy explosion of elements. Serve with fried or steamed rice and your choice of accompanying sauces, such as Soyabi Sauce, ponzu sauce, or Chile-Garlic Sauce.

Serves 4   **Prep time: 30 minutes**

Heat rating:

1 ¹/₂ pounds Japanese eggplant, cut crosswise into ¹/₂-inch-thick slices

¹/₂ pound fresh mung bean sprouts

2 tablespoons rice wine vinegar

2 tablespoons Soyabi Sauce or soy sauce

1 tablespoon toasted sesame oil

1 teaspoon sugar

¹/₂ teaspoon crushed red pepper flakes

3 tablespoons vegetable oil

4 green onions, white part only, thinly sliced

2 fresh Thai chiles, stemmed, seeded, and finely minced

1 red bell pepper, seeded and coarsely chopped

1 green bell pepper, seeded and coarsely chopped

 Rinse and pat dry the eggplant and bean sprouts and set aside. In a large bowl, stir the vinegar, Soyabi Sauce, sesame oil, sugar, and pepper flakes until well mixed. Toss the eggplant and bean sprouts in the vinegar mixture.

Heat the oil in a sauté pan or wok over medium heat, but do not allow it to smoke. Stir-fry the eggplant and bean sprouts until crisp-tender, 4 to 6 minutes. Remove and set aside. Add the green onions, chiles, and bell peppers to the pan and stir-fry until crisp-tender, about 5 minutes. Return the eggplant and bean sprouts to the pan and heat through. Transfer to a serving dish and serve immediately.

Did you know that eggplants are part of the nightshade family, just like tomatoes and potatoes? That, of course, would make it a fruit. This fruit becomes more bitter with age (like the rest of us), so use it in the first day or two after purchasing or picking.

Dr. Mojo's Plastic Surgery Potatoes

Brined Potatoes with Mojo Sauce

Down in the Caribbean islands there are as many variations of mojo sauce as there are people who cook it. See if you like this one which is served with potatoes so wrinkled that they look like they need a face lift.

Serves 4   **Prep time: 45 minutes or less**

Heat rating:

MOJO SAUCE
1 whole head of garlic, peeled and
  crushed
$^1/_4$ teaspoon dried oregano
1 tablespoon ground cumin
1 fresh habanero chile, stemmed,
  seeded, and chopped
2 fresh cayenne chiles, stemmed,
  seeded, and chopped

3 tablespoons rice vinegar, plus
  additional as needed
1 cup extra virgin olive oil
Salt

1 pound very small Yukon gold potatoes
$^1/_4$ cup salt, plus additional as needed

To prepare the sauce, place the garlic, oregano, cumin, chiles, and vinegar in a blender. With the blender running, slowly pour in the oil in a thin stream until blended. Add additional vinegar, to taste, if desired. Season with salt to taste. The sauce can be kept in an airtight container in the refrigerator for up to 2 days.

To prepare the potatoes, wash the potatoes, but leave the skins on. Put them in a pot, cover with cold water, and add the salt. Taste the water; this only works if it tastes as salty as the saltiest sea water you can imagine; add additional salt if necessary. Bring to a boil and cook until the potatoes are tender, about 20 minutes. They will be wrinkled on the outside and tender inside.

To serve, place the Mojo Sauce in a serving bowl in the center of a serving platter and arrange the potatoes around the bowl.

Alternate use for Insanity Sauce #1: Forget those infomercials for high-tech cleaning solutions; several people have reported that Insanity Sauce cleans spots off their driveways. One lady swears by it as an industrial grill cleaner. A customer named Philip advises that while Insanity Sauce is good for sink and tub rust stains, it does not make a good aftershave.

Roly Poly Escarole
Sautéed Escarole

The nutty flavor of the sautéed garlic in this recipe works great with the bitterness of the escarole and the heat of the chiles.

Serves 2 to 3 **Prep time: 10 minutes**

Heat rating:

1 head escarole
1 1/2 tablespoons canola oil
2 cloves garlic, finely chopped

2 fresh red serrano chiles, stemmed, seeded, and minced
Salt

Clean the escarole and separate into leaves. Tear the leaves in half crosswise.

In a sauté pan heat the oil. Add the garlic and sauté until golden brown. Add the chiles and cook about 30 seconds, just until they are fragrant. Add the escarole and sauté just until the leaves begin to shrink. Season with salt to taste and continue to cook, stirring, until the leaves release their moisture, 2 to 3 minutes. Remove from the heat so as not to scorch. Transfer to a serving bowl and serve hot.

Alternate use for Insanity Sauce #2: A man named Dirk put Insanity Sauce on his steak to keep his cat, Tiger, away. He videotaped his cat eating it and then looking into the camera and meowing pitifully.

Barking Puppies
Hush Puppies

These aren't those little lap dogs that double as replacements for mop heads. These are the pit bull variety. Get your rabies shot and bring your appetite. While you're at it, you might want to have a pint of ice cream ready (see page 123). This version of hush puppies is tasty but sure has a bite. To grind the chile de árbol and the dried habanero (both of which are available in the Latin section of most supermarkets), use an electric spice grinder or a mortar and pestle.

Serves a whole heck of a lot—1 selfish cook or 10 polite people

Prep time: 30 minutes or less

Heat rating:

2 cups yellow cornmeal
1 teaspoon ground dried chile de árbol or ground cayenne pepper
1 teaspoon Insanity Spice or dried habanero chile flakes
1 cup all-purpose flour
1 teaspoon baking powder
1 teaspoon salt

1 shallot, finely chopped
3 cloves garlic, minced
1 bunch chives, finely chopped
2 tablespoons butter or solid vegetable shortening, melted
1 cup buttermilk
2 eggs, lightly beaten
Vegetable oil, for deep-frying

In a large bowl, combine the cornmeal, ground chile, Insanity Spice, flour, baking powder, and salt. Mix in the shallot, garlic, chives, shortening, buttermilk, and eggs. Stir together until smooth and all of the flour and cornmeal is incorporated. Let rest for 5 minutes.

Preheat the oven to 250°F and line a large baking sheet with paper towels.

In a deep pot or deep-fryer, heat 2 inches of oil to 375°F. When the oil is hot, drop the batter by the tablespoonful into the oil and brown on all sides, about 2 minutes. Transfer with a slotted spoon to the prepared baking sheet to drain. Taste one and see if you want to share them, but either way, serve them hot. (The hush puppies may be made 15 minutes ahead of serving and kept warm in a 250°F oven.)

Alternate use for Insanity Sauce #3: An Insanity user put the sauce on his terrarium to keep his bird from bothering his turtle. The bird started to make its first trip over to the terrarium to bug the turtle. Upon pecking the Insanity Sauce, the bird jumped back to its cage and yelled "asshole."

Rabid Rabe

Spicy Broccoli Rabe

If the Italians love broccoli rabe, shouldn't you? It is such a waste that it is often used as animal fodder in the United States. Once you blanch out the bitterness, this is a very tasty vegetable and makes a nice accompaniment to grilled chicken or fish dishes.

Serves 4   **Prep time: 25 minutes**

Heat rating:

1 ¹/₂ pounds broccoli rabe, cut in half and hollow stems trimmed
1 cup nonfat chicken broth
1 red bell pepper, seeded and cut into thin strips

¹/₂ to ³/₄ teaspoon crushed red pepper flakes
3 cloves garlic, crushed
Salt and freshly ground black pepper

Bring a pot of water to a rapid boil. Add the broccoli and cook for 3 minutes. Drain. In a large saucepan over medium-high heat, combine the broccoli, chicken broth, bell pepper, pepper flakes, garlic, and salt and pepper to taste and bring to a boil. Decrease the heat to medium and simmer, covered, stirring occasionally, until the vegetables are just tender, about 8 minutes.

Alternate use for Insanity Sauce #4: A priest in California gave a sermon on absolute truth. In his sermon he said, "Insanity Sauce is hot" as an example of truth.

Louisiana Love
Spicy Red Beans and Rice

This is one of those side dishes that is just fine as your whole meal. Use as a bed for grilled or fried fish or chicken.

Serves 6   **Prep time: 45 minutes**

Heat rating:

2 cups water
1 cup long-grain white rice
6 tablespoons chopped fresh thyme or 2 tablespoons dried
1 1/2 teaspoons ground cayenne pepper
2 cups drained canned kidney beans

2 cups chopped green bell pepper (about 3 small bell peppers)
2 cups chopped seeded plum tomatoes (about 4 tomatoes)
1/2 cup bottled Italian dressing
Salt and freshly ground black pepper

Combine the water, rice, 2 tablespoons of the thyme (fresh or dried), and the cayenne in a heavy saucepan over medium-high heat and bring to a boil. Immediately cover the pan, reduce the heat to low, and cook until the rice is tender and the water is absorbed, about 20 minutes.

Transfer the rice to a large bowl. Add the beans, bell peppers, tomatoes, Italian dressing, and remaining 4 tablespoons fresh thyme. Toss to combine. Season the salad to taste with salt and pepper. Serve warm or at room temperature.

Alternate use for Insanity Sauce #5: A farmer stopped his chickens from eating their own eggs by using Insanity Sauce.

Popcorn Puddin'
Cheesy Polenta with Green Chiles

Although polenta can often taste like a cross between wallpaper paste, poi, and cornmeal, it is capable of great things. In this delicious side dish the Italian staple picks up the flavor of cheese, chiles, and fresh corn. Serve this with enchiladas or pork chops. You might want to throw in some roasted bell peppers or sriracha-style sauce or Garlic-Chile Sauce for an extra boost.

Serves 8   Prep time: 45 minutes, plus 25 minutes baking

Heat rating:

2 cups milk
1 cup water
3/4 cup yellow cornmeal
3 cloves garlic, minced
1 teaspoon salt
Freshly ground black pepper
1/2 cup freshly grated Parmesan cheese

1 (7-ounce) can whole green chiles, drained
1 cup drained canned corn kernels
2/3 cup chopped fresh cilantro
2 cups grated Monterey Jack cheese
1/2 cup whipping cream

Preheat the oven to 400°F. Butter an 8 by 8 by 2-inch glass baking dish. Mix together the milk, water, cornmeal, garlic, and salt in a heavy saucepan. Bring to a simmer over medium heat, whisking constantly. Cook until the cornmeal is tender and thickens, stirring often, about 12 minutes. Season with additional salt, if needed, and pepper. Stir in the Parmesan.

Pour half of the polenta into the prepared dish. Cover with half of the chiles and 1/2 cup of the corn kernels. Sprinkle with 1/3 cup of the cilantro and 1 cup of the Jack cheese. Drizzle with 1/4 cup of the cream. Spoon the remaining polenta over the top. Cover with remaining chiles, corn, cilantro, and cheese. Pour the remaining 1/4 cup cream over. (Can be prepared up to this point 1 day ahead. Chill.) Bake until the polenta puffs and begins to brown, 25 to 30 minutes. Cut into squares and serve.

Alternate use for Insanity Sauce #6: We don't think these are in the *New England Journal of Medicine,* but you could learn a lot from Dave's Gourmet customers. Brian writes that putting Insanity Sauce on his rice cured his sinus infection. A stuttering man from New York reveals that Insanity Sauce keeps his conversations going. Julian tells us that Insanity Sauce halted his bronchitis dead in its tracks. Dave in Connecticut says that it is good for everything from headaches to the flu—his secret is to put it in his spaghetti sauce.

Spears and Seeds

Sesame Asparagus

My wife loves it, my two-year-old loves it, and so do I. Doesn't everybody love asparagus? If you don't, this recipe will make you a convert. Toasted sesame oil and seeds provide just the right nutty flavor and crunch to complement the asparagus.

Serves 4   Prep time: 25 minutes

Heat rating:

1 pound fresh asparagus, ends trimmed and cut diagonally into thirds
$^1/_2$ teaspoon vegetable oil
$^1/_2$ cup finely diced red bell pepper

$^1/_2$ teaspoon crushed red pepper flakes
1 tablespoon low-sodium soy sauce
$^1/_2$ teaspoon toasted sesame oil
2 teaspoons sesame seeds, toasted

Cook the asparagus in large pot of boiling salted water until crisp-tender, about 3 minutes. Drain. Rinse the asparagus under cold water. Drain well. (Can be prepared 1 day ahead. Wrap in paper towels and chill.)

Heat the vegetable oil in a large, nonstick skillet over medium-high heat. Add the bell pepper and pepper flakes and stir 1 minute. Add the cooked asparagus and sauté until heated through, about 2 minutes. Add the soy sauce and sesame oil; toss until the asparagus and bell peppers are coated, about 1 minute. Transfer to a serving platter. Sprinkle with the sesame seeds.

Alternate use for Insanity Sauce #7: A billboard owner has reported that strategic placements of Insanity Sauce stops birds from perching on his billboards.

Penang Pasta
Spicy Pasta—Asian Style

Dishes like this are great. They are light, healthy, and packed with flavor. You can also add cooked shrimp, chicken, or sliced beef to it and you've got an easy entrée.

Serves 6   **Prep time: 35 minutes**

Heat rating:

1 pound dried linguine, broken in half
4 tablespoons toasted sesame oil
3 tablespoons honey
3 tablespoons soy sauce
3 tablespoons balsamic vinegar
2 teaspoons Asian garlic-chile paste
3 red bell peppers, seeded and thinly sliced

3 cups snow peas, stringed
1 large red onion, thinly sliced
3/4 cup honey-roasted peanuts, coarsely chopped
1/2 cup chopped fresh basil
1/4 cup sliced green onions, white part only

Cook the pasta in a large pot of boiling salted water until tender but still firm to bite, about 7 minutes, stirring occasionally. Drain very well. Transfer to a large serving bowl.

Whisk 3 tablespoons of the sesame oil, the honey, soy sauce, vinegar, and chile paste in a small bowl to blend. Mix half of the dressing into the pasta. Heat the remaining 1 tablespoon oil in a large pot over medium-high heat. Add the bell peppers, peas, and red onion and sauté until just beginning to wilt, about 2 minutes. Add the bell pepper mixture to the pasta, along with the peanuts, basil, and green onions and enough of the dressing to thoroughly coat all of the ingredients. Toss to combine.

Alternate use for Insanity Sauce #8: Catherine, in Ohio, tells us that Insanity Sauce keeps the Japanese beetles off her roses, and Kevin, in Pittsburgh, has no more problems with deer violating his shrubs after dousing the plants with Insanity Sauce.

Arroza Sabrosa
Tex-Mex Rice

Rice is the bedrock of many good meals. This dish has a number of great flavors that combine to produce a super dish. Add diced sausage and/or chicken and you can serve this as a main course.

Serves 6   **Prep time: 35 minutes**

Heat rating:

2 tablespoons unsalted butter
1 cup chopped onion
1 green bell pepper, seeded and chopped
3 cloves garlic, chopped
2 (6-ounce) packages long-grain and wild rice mix (reserve seasoning packets for another use)

¹/₂ tablespoon ground chile powder
1 (15-ounce) can tomato sauce
¹/₂ cup chopped fresh cilantro
3 cups chicken broth, heated
1 teaspoon Hurtin' Habanero Hot Sauce or other Louisiana-style hot sauce

Melt the butter in a heavy, large saucepan over medium heat. Add the onion, bell pepper, and garlic and sauté until just soft, about 8 minutes. Add the rice and chile powder and stir until well blended, about 1 minute. Mix in the tomato sauce and heat through. Mix in ¹/₄ cup of the cilantro. Pour in the broth and bring the mixture to boil. Cover and reduce the heat to low. Simmer until the rice is tender and the liquid is absorbed, about 12 minutes.

Transfer the rice to a serving bowl. Sprinkle with the hot sauce and garnish with the remaining ¹/₄ cup of cilantro.

Alternate use for Insanity Sauce #9: Dawn, from Virginia, reports that bears stay away from chicken wings slathered with Insanity Sauce.

Frito's Rice
Sofrito Rice

Sofrito is a classic Spanish flavoring sauce. The adaption used in this recipe doesn't have the traditional pork and has been spiced up with chile paste. For a meatier flavor, add some diced bacon when cooking the vegetables.

Serves 4   **Prep time: 45 minutes**

Heat rating:

SOFRITO
3 tablespoons minced onion
3 tablespoons minced red or green bell
  pepper
3 tablespoons chopped fresh cilantro
  sprigs
1 teaspoon Asian garlic-chile paste

3 small cloves garlic, minced
5 teaspoons olive oil

$^1/_2$ teaspoon turmeric
1 $^1/_2$ cups long-grain rice
3 cups water
1 teaspoon salt

To prepare the sofrito, in a 1 $^1/_2$-quart heavy saucepan cook the onion, bell pepper, cilantro, chile paste, and garlic in the oil over moderately low heat, stirring, until the vegetables are soft, about 5 minutes.

Add the turmeric to the sofrito and cook, stirring, 30 seconds. Stir in the rice, water, and salt and bring to a boil, uncovered. Boil uncovered, without stirring, until the surface of rice is covered with steam holes and the grains on top appear dry. Reduce the heat to as low as possible and cook the rice, tightly covered, 15 minutes longer. Remove from the heat and let the rice stand, covered, for 5 minutes before serving.

Alternate use for Insanity Sauce #10: A fellow named Luke and his uncle put Insanity Sauce on a piece of cheese for a mousetrap. That pesky mouse doesn't bother their house any more. . . .

Sugar and Spice
Whipped Chipotle Sweet Potatoes

Fill up the bathtub with this dish, dive in, and eat your way out. This is the side dish that steals the show. You take seconds and thirds and leave your main course sitting on your plate. In addition, it is virtually impossible to cook incorrectly.

Serves 6   **Prep time: 25 minutes, plus 2 hours baking and cooling time**

Heat rating:

5 1/2 pounds sweet potatoes (about 8 large potatoes), scrubbed

1 1/2 to 2 canned chipotle chiles in adobo sauce, minced and mashed to a paste (about 1 tablespoon)

3 tablespoons unsalted butter, cut into pieces and softened

1 teaspoon maple sugar or maple syrup boiled down to crystals (see note)

Salt and freshly ground black pepper

Preheat the oven to 450°F and line a baking sheet with aluminum foil.

Prick the potatoes and place them on the baking sheet. Bake in the middle of the oven 1 to 1 1/2 hours, or until very soft. Cool the potatoes until they can be handled, then scoop the flesh into a bowl. With an electric mixer, beat the potatoes with the chile paste, butter, sugar, and salt and pepper to taste just until smooth. Spread the potatoes in a buttered shallow 2-quart baking dish. (The potatoes may be prepared up to this point 1 day ahead and chilled, covered. Bring the potatoes to room temperature before proceeding.)

Reduce the oven temperature to 350°F. Place the baking dish in the middle of the oven and bake until hot, 20 to 25 minutes.

Maple sugar is about twice as sweet as regular sugar. Maple syrup is made by boiling down maple sap to remove enough water to create a thick syrup. If you keep boiling down the syrup until the liquid is pretty much gone, then you have maple sugar.

No Stuffed Shirts
Chile Cornbread Stuffing I

Stuff your bowl, stuff your mouth, and stuff your neighbor in the closet so he can't eat your stuffing. This dish won't make you a nicer person, but it tastes great. Use this delicious stuffing to stuff poultry (see page 70) or as a side dish with just about anything.

Serves 8

Prep time: 45 minutes to make cornbread; 30 minutes to prep, 50 minutes to bake stuffing

Heat rating:

CORNBREAD
2 cups yellow cornmeal
2 cups all-purpose flour
1/2 cup sugar
2 tablespoons baking powder
2 teaspoons salt
2 cups milk
2/3 cup vegetable oil
2 large eggs

STUFFING
1 pound chorizo sausage, casings removed
2 1/4 cups chopped onions (about 2 large onions)
2 red bell peppers, seeded and chopped
1 fresh Anaheim chile, seeded and chopped
1/4 cup chopped fresh cilantro
1 1/2 teaspoons dried oregano
2/3 cup low-salt chicken broth

To prepare the cornbread, preheat the oven to 400°F. Butter a shallow 9-inch-square glass baking dish. In a large bowl, combine the cornmeal, flour, sugar, baking powder, and salt. In a medium bowl, whisk the milk, oil, and eggs. Add the milk mixture to the dry ingredients and stir just until blended. Transfer the batter to the prepared baking dish. Bake until a toothpick inserted into the center comes out clean, about 25 minutes. Cool. (The corn bread can be prepared up to 2 days in advance. Cover and refrigerate until serving or using in stuffing.)

To prepare the stuffing, preheat the oven to 375°F. Cut the cornbread into 1/2-inch cubes (you'll need 12 cups). Transfer to a baking sheet. Bake until cornbread cubes are dry but not hard, about 15 minutes. Transfer to a large bowl.

Butter a 9 by 13-inch glass baking dish. Cook the chorizo in large skillet over medium-high heat until browned and crumbly, about 10 minutes. Reduce the heat to medium-low. Add the onions, bell peppers, and chile and sauté until tender, about 15 minutes. Stir the chorizo mixture, cilantro, and oregano into the cornbread. Mix in enough of the broth to moisten the bread. Spoon into the prepared baking dish. Cover with buttered foil, buttered side down. (The stuffing may be prepared up to this point 1 to 2 days ahead and covered and chilled.) Bake in a preheated 375°F oven until heated through, about 50 minutes. Serve warm.

Pining and Combining
Chile Cornbread Stuffing II

With the combination of pine nuts, tequila, and marjoram, this dish is just like most of the dishes Americans cook every day. I have trouble getting past breakfast without the trio. Seriously, don't miss this stuffing, it will make you give thanks.

Serves 8

Prep time: 45 minutes to make cornbread, plus 30 minutes prep, plus 50 minutes cooking time

Heat rating:

Cornbread (page 69)

1 cup raisins

¹/₃ cup tequila

6 tablespoons butter

2 large fresh poblano chiles, roasted, peeled, stemmed, seeded, and chopped

2 cups chopped onions (about 2 large onions)

1 ¹/₂ tablespoons chopped fresh thyme

³/₄ teaspoon dried marjoram, crumbled

³/₄ teaspoon dried rubbed sage

¹/₂ pound sourdough bread, crust trimmed and cut into ¹/₂-inch cubes (about 4 cups)

³/₄ cup pine nuts, lightly toasted

Salt and freshly ground black pepper

2 large eggs, beaten

1 ¹/₄ cups low-salt chicken broth (optional)

Make and the cool cornbread from Chile Cornbread Stuffing I.

Combine the raisins and tequila in saucepan over medium heat and simmer 5 minutes. Remove from the heat. Let stand until most of the tequila is absorbed, stirring occasionally, about 2 hours. Drain well.

Melt the butter in large sauté pan over medium heat. Add the chiles, onions, thyme, marjoram, and sage. Cook until the onion just begins to brown, stirring occasionally, about 10 minutes. Transfer to a large bowl.

Crumble the cornbread into the bowl and add the raisins, sourdough bread cubes, and pine nuts. Toss to blend. Season the stuffing to taste with salt and pepper. Mix the eggs into the stuffing.

To cook the stuffing outside of a turkey: Preheat the oven to 350°F. Generously butter a 9 by 13-inch glass baking dish. Add enough of the broth to the stuffing to lightly moisten it. Transfer the stuffing to the baking dish. Cover with buttered foil, buttered side down; bake until heated through, about 30 minutes. Uncover and bake until the top is crisp and golden, about 15 minutes longer. To cook the stuffing in a turkey: Loosely fill the main turkey cavity with the stuffing immediately before cooking. Roast your turkey until the meat reaches an internal temperature of 165°F. Store the stuffing separately in the refrigerator if any leftovers survive.

Grit It Out
Roasted Pepper Grits

You don't get much more southern than this. Grits are one of those great comfort foods, like polenta or oatmeal, which aren't great by themselves, but when doctored up with the right stuff, become really satisfying. Try this recipe with a plate of eggs and bacon or just by itself.

Serves 6   **Prep time: 20 minutes, plus 35 minutes cooking time**

Heat rating:

2 medium red bell peppers, roasted, peeled, stemmed, and seeded
1 large onion, finely chopped
2 tablespoons unsalted butter
1 tablespoon minced garlic
1 cup quick-cooking grits

4 cups whole milk
1 cup water
3/4 teaspoon Cool Cayenne Pepper Sauce or other Louisiana-style hot sauce
Salt and freshly ground black pepper

In a food processor or blender, purée the roasted peppers until smooth. In a large saucepan, sauté the onion in the butter over moderately low heat, stirring, until soft, about 5 minutes. Add the garlic and cook, stirring, 2 minutes. Stir in the grits and then add 2 cups of the milk in a stream, while stirring constantly. Simmer the mixture, stirring, until the milk is absorbed, about 5 minutes. Stir in the remaining 2 cups milk and simmer, stirring occasionally, until the milk is absorbed, about 5 minutes. Stir in the water and simmer uncovered, stirring occasionally, until the grits are soft and thickened, about 35 minutes.

Stir in the roasted pepper purée, hot sauce, and salt and pepper to taste. Transfer to a serving bowl and serve.

The grits may also be made 1 day ahead and chilled, covered, in a buttered 10-inch, 6-cup shallow baking dish. Reheat the grits in a 400°F oven until hot, about 15 minutes.

Grits, also called hominy grits, are a gift from the Native Americans. Hominy is corn with the husk and germ removed by soaking the corn in slaked lime or lye. The hominy is then ground to make grits. Grits can also be made from ground oats or rice.

Mr. Toad's Spicy Ride
Roasted Mushrooms with Tomatillo Salsa

Shrooms—and I don't mean the psychedelic kind—are one of those vegetables that you either love or hate. I love mushrooms, especially portobello mushrooms, and especially with garlic. If you add Insanity Sauce to this recipe make sure that your kitchen is well ventilated. You can also make a mini version of this recipe by using cremini mushrooms instead of portobellos.

Serves 4   **Prep time: 30 minutes**

Heat rating: **(with Insanity Sauce)**

ROASTED GARLIC VINAIGRETTE
1 head garlic
1 teaspoon olive oil
Salt and freshly ground black pepper
1/3 cup apple cider vinegar
1 cup Roasted Chile Oil (page 33)

2 cloves garlic, chopped
1 cup boiling water
Salt and freshly ground black pepper
3 to 4 drops Insanity Sauce (optional)
1/2 cup fresh cilantro leaves, very finely chopped

TOMATILLO SALSA
10 fresh tomatillos
2 fresh green Anaheim chiles, stemmed and chopped
1 green habanero chile, stemmed, seeded, and chopped (use 3 habaneros if you don't use Insanity Sauce)

4 large portobello mushrooms, stems and ribs gently removed with a teaspoon
2 teaspoons olive oil
Salt and freshly ground black pepper

 To prepare the vinaigrette, preheat the oven to 350°F. Cut off the top third of the head of garlic—do not peel the garlic cloves. Place the garlic in a small roasting pan and pour the olive oil over the top of the cloves until well coated. Lightly sprinkle the garlic with salt and pepper. Place the garlic in the oven and roast until dark golden brown and soft, 45 minutes to 1 hour. Remove and cool. Into a blender, gently squeeze the bottom of the garlic cloves until the flesh pops out from the husks; discard the husks. Pour in the vinegar and begin blending. With the blender running, slowly drizzle in the chile oil. Transfer to a serving bowl, cover, and set aside.

Preheat the oven to 375°F, prepare a fire in a charcoal grill, or preheat a gas grill to medium heat.

To prepare the salsa, husk and rinse the tomatillos. In a food processor, blend the tomatillos, chiles, and garlic. Transfer to a microwavable serving bowl. Stir the boiling water into the tomatillo-chile mixture. Season to taste with salt and pepper, and stir in the Insanity Sauce and the cilantro. Cover and set aside.

Place the mushroom caps, open side up, on a nonstick baking sheet. Drizzle with the olive oil and lightly season with salt and pepper. If cooking in the oven, roast until the mushrooms have released their moisture and are cooked through, about 12 minutes.

If grilling, begin with the mushrooms open side up; grill over low to medium heat. As the mushrooms release their moisture, gently flip with tongs. Cook about 15 minutes, until soft.

Warm the salsa in the microwave. Serve the mushrooms alongside the bowls of salsa and vinaigrette for dipping or drizzling.

When you burn (or desensitize) the taste buds in your mouth from heat or from foods that are too spicy, they do come back. Spicy foods do not destroy taste buds. They don't actually burn you but act upon the same pain receptors as heat. This is why they seem to burn.

Entrées to Agony

Zebra Fish in a Shell
Grilled Fish Tacos   78

Scallops with a Wallop
Sea Scallops in Habanero-Berry
Sauce   79

Schizophrenic Hens
Cornish Hens in Jalapeño-Apple
Sauce   80

Balmy Beans and Rice
Beans and Rice in Coconut Milk   81

Piquant Pig in Paradise
Pork Chops with Mango Sauce   82

Puckering Chicken Lips
Tangy Grilled Chicken Breasts   83

**Mary Had a Spicy Lamb (Mary Also
Had a Black Sheep)**
Lamb Stew   84

Crazy Cajun Salmon
Cajun Salmon with Chile-Herb
Butter   85

Batter Up, Shrimp
Tempura Shrimp with Grilled
Vegetables and Soba Noodles   86

Uncle Fez-ter's Chicken Pie
Bastilla   88

Marco Polo's Buried Treasure
Asian Chile Pesto Sauce with
Linguine   89

A Pig with a Drawl
Piquant Southern Pork Roast   90

A Berry Good Piggy
Cranberry-Jalapeño Pork Loin   91

Fireball Shrimp
Fried Pepper Shrimp   92

Hot Cha Cha Chops
Roasted Lamb Chops with Scotch
Bonnets and Sage   112

Kung Fu Chicken
Cashew-Chicken Stir-Fry   113

Balls of Fire
Meatball Soup   114

Shmokin' Shrimp
Shrimp with Chipotle-Orange
Glaze   115

Chicken à la Hash
Chicken-Chile Hash   116

Chicken Dijonotle
Grilled Chicken with Dijon-
Chipotle Sauce   117

Mr. McDonald's Secret Burger
Green Chile Cheeseburger with
Roasted Red Pepper Ketchup   118

Pig in a Burgundy Blanket
Pork Roast with Chile Colorado
(Red Sauce)   120

Zebra Fish in a Shell
Grilled Fish Tacos

This is a Southern California staple. Saying "Dude, these are excellent," is optional. It may be helpful to be in the right frame of mind to eat these. Repeat after me, "radical," "bitchin'," and "awesome." I love fish tacos and used to experiment with them when I owned a restaurant called Burrito Madness. They are so light and fresh. I like mine with salsa and guacamole and, of course, hot sauce.

Serves 4   Prep time: 20 to 30 minutes

Heat rating:

1 1/2 pounds fresh red snapper or mahi mahi fillets
Juice of 4 limes
1/4 cup water
Pinch of salt
Olive oil, for brushing
1 dozen 6- to 8-inch tortillas (preferably corn but you can use flour)
1 lime, halved

3 fresh jalapeño chiles, thinly sliced crosswise
Crazy Caribbean Sauce or Caribbean-style hot sauce
Chopped vegetables (such as carrots, napa cabbage, and cucumber), for garnish (optional)
1 bunch cilantro, stemmed and chopped, for garnish (optional)

Prepare a fire in a charcoal grill or preheat a gas grill to medium-high heat. Marinate the fish in the lime juice, water, and a pinch of salt for 10 minutes. Drain, then brush both sides of each fillet lightly with olive oil.

Grill the fish, turning once, for 10 minutes, until firm and opaque. While the fish is grilling, warm the tortillas on the grill until hot. Make tacos by cutting the fish into cubes and placing in hot tortillas. Finish the tacos off with a squeeze of lime, some chile slices, and hot sauce to taste. You may also want to add any type of chopped veggies and cilantro as a garnish.

Scallops with a Wallop
Sea Scallops in Habanero-Berry Sauce

If you are having company over they will really appreciate this gourmet dish, except for one thing: OUCH.

Serves 4   Prep time: 40 minutes

Heat rating:

HABANERO-BERRY SAUCE
3 tablespoons butter
3 tablespoons sugar
$^1/_3$ cup dry white wine
$^1/_3$ cup freshly squeezed orange juice
2 tablespoons raspberry vinegar
1 or 2 fresh habanero chiles, seeded and minced
1 $^1/_4$ cups fresh or frozen blackberries
1 $^1/_4$ cups beef broth
$^1/_2$ cup low-salt chicken broth

2 tablespoons brandy
1 tablespoon maple syrup

1 teaspoon vegetable oil
1 teaspoon peeled minced fresh gingerroot
16 to 20 (about 1 pound) jumbo sea scallops
Salt and freshly ground black pepper
Fresh blackberries, for garnish

To prepare the sauce, melt 2 tablespoons of the butter in a heavy nonstick pan over medium-high heat. Add the sugar and stir for about 5 minutes, or until the sugar turns amber in color. Mix in the wine, orange juice, and vinegar and bring to a boil, stirring constantly. Add the chiles, berries, and both broths and boil until the sauce is reduced to about 1 cup, stirring occasionally. Strain the sauce through a sieve into a saucepan, pressing out all of the juices. Stir in the brandy and maple syrup, and then set aside.

Heat the oil in a frying pan over medium heat. When hot, add the ginger and cook for 2 minutes, stirring frequently. Add the scallops and cook, continuing to stir often, for 4 to 5 minutes, or until firm and opaque.

Meanwhile, warm the sauce over medium heat and stir in the remaining 1 tablespoon of butter. Add salt and pepper to taste. For each serving, spoon about $^1/_4$ cup of the sauce onto a plate and place 4 to 5 scallops over the sauce. Garnish each plate with fresh blackberries.

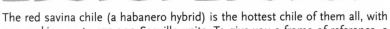

The red savina chile (a habanero hybrid) is the hottest chile of them all, with one ranking up to 577,000 Scoville units. To give you a frame of reference, a jalapeño usually has about 2,000 to 4,000 Scoville units.

Schizophrenic Hens
Cornish Hens in Jalapeño-Apple Sauce

Due to language problems, it may be difficult to actually diagnose chickens, but the sauce in this recipe is sure to cure what ails them . . . and you! Game hens are a succulent treat. If you want something with more game, try pigeon (not the city-dwelling kind) or squab.

Serves 4   **Prep time: 45 minutes or less**

Heat rating:

JALAPEÑO-APPLE SAUCE
1/2 cup apple jelly
1 1/2 tablespoons freshly squeezed
   lemon juice
1 1/2 tablespoons freshly squeezed
   lime juice
1 tablespoon Worcestershire sauce
1 teaspoon minced drained pickled
   jalapeño chile

4 Cornish hens (1 1/4 to 1 1/2 pounds
   each), halved and backbones
   discarded
Salt and freshly ground black pepper
Couscous or rice, for serving

 Preheat the oven to 500°F. Line a roasting pan with foil and set a rack flat inside the pan.

To prepare the sauce, combine the apple jelly, lemon and lime juices, Worcestershire sauce, and chile in a saucepan and heat the mixture over moderate heat, stirring, until the jelly is just melted, about 4 minutes. Set aside.

Pat the Cornish hens dry, sprinkle them with salt and pepper, and arrange the halves, skin sides down, on the rack in the roasting pan. Brush the halves with some of the sauce and roast them in the lower third of the oven for 15 minutes. Baste the halves with the sauce, turn them over, and continue roasting for 7 minutes longer. Baste the hens again and roast another 7 minutes, or until the juices run clear when a thigh is pricked with a skewer. Serve on a bed of couscous or rice.

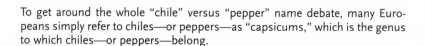

To get around the whole "chile" versus "pepper" name debate, many Europeans simply refer to chiles—or peppers—as "capsicums," which is the genus to which chiles—or peppers—belong.

Balmy Beans and Rice
Beans and Rice in Coconut Milk

For the thinking impaired, this is not a balm that you rub on your skin. "Balmy" refers to the warming effect of chiles and the tropical flavor lent by the coconut milk in this dish. It hits the spot almost as well as a good bar of chocolate.

Serves 4   **Prep time: 45 minutes**

Heat rating:

2 1/2 cups vegetable broth
1 (15-ounce) can kidney beans, drained (use "low sodium" if possible)
1 cup canned unsweetened regular or light coconut milk
1 fresh jalapeño chile, seeded and minced

1 teaspoon dried thyme
1/4 teaspoon ground allspice
3/4 cup medium-grain white rice
1 cup thinly sliced green onions, white part only
Salt and freshly ground black pepper

Combine 2 cups of the vegetable broth, the kidney beans, coconut milk, chile, thyme, and allspice in large, heavy saucepan. Bring the mixture to a boil over medium-high heat. Stir in the rice. Reduce the heat to medium-low and simmer the mixture uncovered until most of liquid is absorbed and the rice is almost tender, stirring often, about 20 minutes.

Mix 3/4 cup of the green onions into the rice. Continue to simmer about 5 minutes longer, until the rice is very tender and the mixture is creamy, adding more broth by 1/4 cupfuls if the mixture seems dry. Season to taste with salt and pepper. Transfer to a serving bowl. Sprinkle with the remaining 1/4 cup green onions and serve.

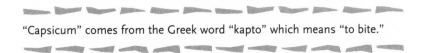

"Capsicum" comes from the Greek word "kapto" which means "to bite."

Piquant Pig in Paradise
Pork Chops with Mango Sauce

I don't know if pigs love fruit, but it tastes super on their chops. There is just some magical relationship between pork and fruit. It is kind of like lamb and mint or Insanity Sauce and pain.

Serves 4   **Prep time: 45 minutes**

Heat rating:

1 small mango, peeled, pitted, and cut into chunks
1 tablespoon plus 2 teaspoons vegetable oil
1 tablespoon minced garlic
1 fresh jalapeño chile, stemmed, seeded, and minced
1/3 cup chopped fresh tarragon

3/4 cup low-salt chicken broth
1 1/2 tablespoons firmly packed light brown sugar
1 tablespoon soy sauce
Salt and freshly ground black pepper
4 (6- to 8-ounce) center-cut pork chops, about 1 inch thick

 Purée the mango in a food processor. Set aside 1/2 cup purée (reserve any remaining purée for another use—it should keep a week or so in the fridge).

Prepare a fire in a charcoal grill, preheat a gas grill to medium high, or preheat a broiler.

Heat the 1 tablespoon oil in a skillet over medium heat. Add the garlic and chile, then the tarragon; sauté about 1 minute, or until they begin to release their juices. Add the broth, brown sugar, and soy sauce. Bring to a boil, stirring occasionally, until the sugar is dissolved. Reduce heat to low and simmer 3 minutes. Gradually whisk in the reserved 1/2 cup mango purée. Simmer until the sauce thickens and coats a spoon, about 5 minutes. Season with salt and pepper to taste and remove from the heat.

Brush the pork chops with the 2 teaspoons oil. Sprinkle with salt and pepper. Grill or broil the chops until just cooked through (no longer pink), about 5 minutes per side. Transfer to plates. Warm the sauce over low heat, stirring occasionally. Drizzle over the chops and serve.

Did you know that brown sugar is just white sugar with added molasses? Did you know that you can soften hardened brown sugar by placing it in a sealed bag with an apple wedge for a day or two? Did you know that your pork chops are burning and you should go save them?

Puckering Chicken Lips
Tangy Grilled Chicken Breasts

Okay, so chickens don't really have lips, but this dish will make *you* pucker up. This is the kind of basic Asian-Mexican cooking that I love—it's healthy, tasty, and easy to make. You can substitute a good crumbly Mexican cheese, such as queso cotija, for the Monterey Jack in this recipe. Serve with black beans, rice, lettuce, salsa, and hot-flour tortillas.

Serves 4   **Prep time: 40 minutes, plus overnight marinating**

Heat rating:

MARINADE

1/4 cup freshly squeezed lime juice
3 tablespoons soy sauce
2 tablespoons vegetable oil
1 tablespoon sugar
1 tablespoon chopped fresh oregano
1/2 tablespoon chopped fresh rosemary

1/2 tablespoon minced garlic
3/4 teaspoons ground chile powder
1/4 teaspoon ground cayenne pepper

4 boneless skinless chicken breast halves
4 ounces Monterey Jack cheese, shredded (optional)

In a bowl, whisk together the lime juice, soy sauce, oil, sugar, oregano, rosemary, garlic, chile powder, and cayenne. Place the chicken in a shallow glass baking dish. Pour the marinade over the chicken, cover, and refrigerate, turning occasionally, for at least 3 hours, or overnight.

Prepare a fire in a charcoal grill or preheat a gas grill to medium-high heat. Remove the chicken breasts from the marinade, discarding the marinade. Grill the chicken, turning occasionally, about 12 minutes, until cooked through (no longer pink and the juices run clear). Transfer the chicken breasts to plates. Sprinkle the cheese on the chicken while hot.

It is commonly said that to kill bacteria, chicken should be cooked to an internal temperature of 165°F. A secret that chefs know is that this will also kill all flavor and make your chicken taste like last summer's flip-flops. Chefs will tell you that if you instead cook chicken to an internal temperature of 145°F, it will be great. The question is, Are you feeling lucky?

Mary Had a Spicy Lamb (Mary Also Had a Black Sheep)
Lamb Stew

No one is safe from the chileheads, not even Mary or her little lamb. This is one of those great hearty family meals—flavorful and succulent with pieces of lamb that just melt in your mouth. If you add Insanity Sauce, not only does the lamb melt, so does your mouth. You may find precut lamb cubes, sometimes labeled "cubes for kebabs" at your local grocery store.

Serves 8   Prep time: 2 hours and 30 minutes (mostly simmering)

Heat rating:  **(with Insanity Sauce)**

2 tablespoons peanut oil
1 3/4 pounds lamb shoulder, trimmed and cut into 1-inch cubes
1 teaspoon minced garlic
2 large onions, chopped
1 (6-ounce) can tomato paste
3 bay leaves
1/4 teaspoon ground cayenne pepper
4 drops Insanity Sauce (optional)
Pinch of salt
Pinch of freshly ground black pepper

1 3/4 cups beef stock or broth
1 3/4 cups water
3/4 cup smooth peanut butter
1 cup diced carrots
4 fresh jalapeño chiles (or 2 habanero chiles, if you like extra heat), halved lengthwise and seeded
1/2 habanero chile, seeded and minced
1 cup shucked fresh or frozen peas
Cooked white rice, as an accompaniment

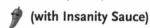 Heat the oil in a large soup pot or Dutch oven over medium-high heat. Add the lamb, garlic, and onions and cook until the lamb is brown, stirring occasionally, about 6 minutes. Mix in the tomato paste, bay leaves, cayenne pepper, and Insanity Sauce and cook 1 minute. Add the salt, pepper, beef stock, and water and bring to boil. Reduce to a simmer and cook until the lamb is tender, about 1 hour and 20 minutes.

Stir the peanut butter, carrots, and chiles into the stew and cook until the carrots are tender, about 30 minutes. Add the peas and cook until heated through. Discard the bay leaves and jalapeño halves. Serve the stew ladled over rice in individual bowls.

Crazy Cajun Salmon
Cajun Salmon with Chile-Herb Butter

Everyone loves salmon. It is such a flavorful fish, especially with all the great herbs and spices included here. Give this recipe a try and it will be Mardi Gras in your mouth.

Serves 4   **Prep time: 35 minutes**

Heat rating:

4 salmon fillets (about 8 ounces each),
   1 to 1 1/2 inches thick

SPICE BLEND

2 teaspoons salt
1 teaspoon ground cayenne pepper
1 teaspoon paprika
1/2 teaspoon white pepper
1/4 teaspoon garlic powder
1/2 teaspoon freshly ground black pepper
1/4 teaspoon dried thyme
1/4 teaspoon dried basil
1 teaspoon crushed red pepper flakes

CHILE-HERB BUTTER

1 cup unsalted butter, at room
   temperature
2 fresh green jalapeño chiles, stemmed,
   seeded, and very finely minced
4 sprigs cilantro, leaves only, finely
   chopped
2 sprigs parsley, leaves only, finely
   chopped

Insanity Seafood Sauce or prepared
   salsa, for serving

Prepare a fire in a charcoal grill or preheat a gas grill to medium-high heat. Prepare the fillets by rinsing them and making sure that all of the bones have been removed and that no skin is left on the edges. Pat the fillets dry and set aside.

Combine all of the spice blend ingredients in a sauté pan and lightly toast over very low heat, stirring constantly, until light brown and aromatic. Transfer from the pan to a shallow dish or plate.

Prepare the herb butter by combining the butter, chiles, and herbs in small bowl and blending with a wooden spoon until smooth and well mixed. Place the butter on a piece of wax paper or plastic wrap, rolling the butter up in a tube shape, 2 inches in diameter. Refrigerate briefly while the fillets are grilling.

To grill the fillets, lightly oil each fillet with canola oil then roll the fillet in the spice blend until uniformly covered. Grill the fillets over medium heat until browned on each side and cooked through to the middle, about 3 minutes per side.

Unroll the tube of butter and allow to soften briefly. Cut the butter crosswise into 1/2-inch-thick rounds. Serve the fillets hot from the grill topped with the herb butter and Insanity Seafood Sauce or your favorite salsa.

Batter Up, Shrimp

Tempura Shrimp with Grilled Vegetables and Soba Noodles

Before you look at the long ingredient list and bunt, understand that this recipe is easy and delicious. It is a very common Japanese dish. If you want to avoid fried foods, you can make a lighter version by skipping the tempura batter and grilling the shrimp instead. Look for the soba noodles in your local supermarket; if they're not there, check your local Asian market.

Serves 4   **Prep time: 50 minutes**

Heat rating:

1/2 cup all-purpose flour
1/2 cup cornstarch
1/4 teaspoon baking soda
1/4 teaspoon turmeric
1/4 teaspoon ground cayenne pepper
1/4 teaspoon yellow curry powder
1 cup club soda
6 green onions, root end trimmed
1 Chinese eggplant or small Italian or globe eggplant, sliced crosswise 1/4 inch thick
2 fresh green Anaheim chiles, stemmed, seeded, and sliced into 1-inch-thick strips

Canola oil, for frying and brushing
4 cups chicken stock or broth
2 (10-ounce) packages dried soba noodles
1 small yellow onion, finely minced
1 teaspoon Garlic-Chile Sauce or Asian garlic-chile paste
2 teaspoons salt
1 teaspoon freshly ground black pepper
1/2 teaspoon ground mace
1 1/2 pounds medium uncooked shrimp, peeled and deveined

In a small mixing bowl, combine the flour, cornstarch, baking soda, turmeric, cayenne, curry powder, and club soda, stirring until smooth. Set aside and keep at room temperature for a minimum of 30 minutes and up to 2 hours.

Prepare a fire in a charcoal grill or preheat a gas grill to medium-high heat. Lightly brush the green onions, eggplant, and chiles with oil and place the vegetables on the grill. Grill for about 5 minutes, turning to grill evenly, until well marked on all sides. Remove from the grill, wrap in aluminum foil, and keep warm in a very low-temperature oven while finishing the dish.

In a large pot, heat the stock over medium heat until gently boiling. Add the noodles, onion, Garlic-Chile Sauce, salt, pepper, and mace and stir until the noodles have separated. Continue to cook the noodles over medium heat until soft, 8 to 10 minutes. Drain and set aside.

Heat 5 inches of canola oil in a deep frying pan or pot to 365°F or until a small drop of water splatters when dropped into the oil. Working in small batches, gently dip the prepared shrimp into the reserved batter and then place them carefully into the oil.

Do not overcrowd the pan as this will slow the cooking process and cause the shrimp to absorb too much oil while frying. Cook the shrimp until golden brown on all sides, about 5 minutes. Remove the shrimp from the oil using a slotted spoon and drain briefly on paper towels.

For each serving, place one-quarter of the noodles into a large soup bowl, top with some of the grilled vegetables as desired, and place 4 to 6 of the shrimp on top of the grilled vegetables.

Scoville units were invented by a gentleman named Wilbur Scoville, almost one hundred years ago. His test was organoleptic, and based on the tasting ability of a trained tasting panel. Each person would taste each chile in dilution and then see how many drops of water it took to neutralize the heat in their mouths. To give you an idea of common Scoville unit measurements, jalapeños rate between 2,000 and 4,000 units, and Insanity Sauce has been measured over 100,000 units.

While Scoville units are still relevant, there are lots of people who have gone to a scale from 1 to 10. The scale works like the Richter scale, with each number being greater than the last by a factor of 10. For the really technical stuff, there is also an HPLC (High-Pressure Liquid Chromatography) test that chemically analyzes capsaicin molecules and roughly translates the result into Scoville units.

It turns out that old Wilbur's scale was pretty good, and that is why chileheads refer to relative heat in Scoville units even today.

Uncle Fez-ter's Chicken Pie
Bastilla

Bastilla is a traditional Moroccan dish usually prepared with pigeon—wild pigeon, not the dirty urban variety! To save you a hunting trip, this recipe uses chicken instead. This dish takes a little time but has such a satisfying, exotic flavor, it's worth it. Serve with Garlic-Cilantro Sauce (page 95) or couscous and currants.

Serves 4   **Prep time: 1 hour and 30 minutes**

Heat rating: **(with Insanity Sauce)**

12 sheets frozen phyllo dough

1/4 cup canola oil, plus additional for brushing phyllo

1 yellow onion, peeled and finely chopped

2 pounds boneless chicken meat, cut into medium cubes

1/2 teaspoon peeled finely minced fresh gingerroot

1 teaspoon ground turmeric powder

2 teaspoons salt

1/2 teaspoon freshly ground black pepper

2 teaspoons ground cinnamon

4 cups chicken stock or broth

6 sprigs fresh cilantro, leaves only, finely chopped

4 sprigs fresh flat-leaf parsley, leaves only, finely chopped

6 eggs

3 drops Insanity Sauce (optional)

Toasted sliced almonds, for garnish (optional)

Preheat the oven to 350°F.

Lay out the phyllo dough on a flat surface and allow to defrost at room temperature, covered loosely with a lightly dampened cloth.

Meanwhile, in a sauté pan, heat the 1/4 cup oil over medium heat and sauté the onions until lightly colored but not brown. Add the chicken, ginger, turmeric, salt, pepper, and cinnamon and sauté until the chicken is cooked through, about 10 minutes. Add the stock and simmer until the liquid is reduced by one-third. Transfer the chicken with a slotted spoon to a large bowl. Stir in the cilantro and parsley and set aside.

Crack the eggs into the sauté pan with the remaining stock and cook, stirring constantly, until they resemble scrambled eggs. Add to the chicken mixture and stir to combine.

Lightly oil a 9 by 13-inch ovenproof baking dish. Line the bottom of the pan with 6 layers of phyllo, lightly brushing the top of the dough with oil between each layer. Spread the chicken filling over the phyllo in an even layer. Top with an additional 6 layers of phyllo dough, brushing with oil between each layer. Brush the top of the phyllo with additional oil, then place in the center of the oven and bake until heated through and the top is crisp, 25 to 30 minutes. Serve topped with toasted almonds, if desired.

Marco Polo's Buried Treasure
Asian Chile Pesto Sauce with Linguine

This dish is much easier to navigate than the early trade routes and it is tasty too. If you like this pesto, you can make extra and serve it over fish or chicken or use it as a bread spread.

Serves 4   **Prep time: 25 minutes**

Heat rating: **(with Insanity Sauce)**

ASIAN CHILE PESTO
1 cup unsalted roasted peanuts
1/2 cup soy sauce
2 drops Insanity Sauce (if you dare!)
4 small dried chiles (such as de árbol or cayenne), softened in 2 cups boiling water and drained
6 sprigs cilantro, leaves only
1/4 cup honey

3/4 cup water
3 cloves garlic, minced
1/2 cup toasted sesame oil
1 pound dried linguine pasta
2 tablespoons cold butter
Toasted peanuts, for garnish
Cilantro leaves, for garnish

To prepare the pesto, place the peanuts in the bowl of a food processor, and process until finely ground. With the motor running, add the soy sauce, Insanity Sauce, chiles, cilantro, honey, water, garlic, and sesame oil. Process until a thick, smooth paste has formed. (The pesto can be transferred to a bowl, covered, and refrigerated up to 24 hours.)

In a large pot of boiling water, cook the pasta until al dente; drain and set aside. To complete the dish, heat the pesto in a large sauté pan over medium heat until simmering. Add thecooked pasta and toss gently, heating through. When the sauce returns to a simmer, add the cold butter and stir in until melted.

Serve the pasta in heated bowls with a chile placed on top of each serving. Garnish with the toasted peanuts and cilantro.

Birds love to eat chiles, and as you can guess, their droppings can be very rich in seeds. In fact, if birds didn't eat so many chiles, we probably wouldn't have so many different varieties everywhere! The strange thing is that birds have the same reaction to grapes as people do to chiles: they seem to experience burning.

A Pig With a Drawl
Piquant Southern Pork Roast

This southern piggy speaks slowly and, evidently, must run slowly (or why would it be dinner?). This is a great meal for entertaining. Serve it with glazed or stewed apples and your taste buds will be singing Dixie. Although the recipe calls for a 3-pound pork roast, to accommodate a larger crowd, simply use a heavier roast and double the braising sauce. For spicier meat, add additional hot pepper sauce and a few drops of vinegar to the sauce.

Serves 8   Prep time: 2 hours

Heat rating:

1 (3-pound) pork shoulder roast
2 tablespoons vegetable oil

BRAISING SAUCE
1 teaspoon celery seeds
1/3 cup apple cider vinegar
1/2 cup ketchup
1/2 teaspoon ground chile powder
1/2 teaspoon ground nutmeg

1 teaspoon packed brown sugar
1/8 teaspoon ground cinnamon
1 bay leaf, crumbled
1/2 teaspoon salt
1/2 teaspoon lemon pepper
4 dashes Hurtin' Jalapeño Sauce or other jalapeño sauce
1 cup water

In a large, heavy skillet, brown the roast on all sides in the oil. Place the roast in a heavy roasting pan with a tight-fitting lid, or in a large baking pan that you can seal with aluminum foil.

Combine all of the braising sauce ingredients in a saucepan and bring to a boil. Boil for 1 minute; pour the mixture over the roast. Cover the pan tightly. Place the roast in a preheated 325°F oven and bake for about 35 to 45 minutes per pound, or until the meat reaches an internal temperature of 165°F. Baste several times with the juices in the pan. Remove the roast and allow to cool slightly. Slice the roast into bite-sized, thin pieces.

In Siberia, there have been reports of people putting chile powder in their socks to warm their feet.

A Berry Good Piggy
Cranberry-Jalapeño Pork Loin

In case you don't want to eat the other white meat, the cranberries will make this look like red meat. If you use fresh cranberries, you might want to add a little bit of honey or sugar to the marinade. I would, but I'm a recovering sugar addict. Serve this with a potato dish of your choice.

Serves 6   **Prep time: 30 minutes, plus marinating time**

Heat rating:

1 (4-pound) pork loin
12 ounces fresh cranberries, or 1 (12-ounce) can whole cranberries
4 fresh red jalapeño chiles, stemmed, seeded, and finely chopped
2 tablespoons canola oil

2 teaspoons salt
$^1/_2$ teaspoon freshly ground black pepper
6 sprigs cilantro, leaves only, finely chopped
$^1/_2$ cup red wine vinegar

Cut the loin into 1-inch-thick steaks. With a sharp knife, butterfly the steaks by halving them horizontally, almost all the way through the meat, but leaving one side still attached (or you can have your butcher prepare these for you). Spread open the steaks in an even layer in the bottom of a large pan. Set aside.

Combine the cranberries, chiles, oil, salt, pepper, cilantro, and vinegar in a small saucepan and heat over medium-high heat to a boil. Lower the heat and simmer until slightly reduced and the cranberries have popped open, about 5 minutes. Mash the cranberries with a fork or potato masher and cool the mixture slightly. Top the loin steaks with the cranberry mixture and refrigerate for a minimum of 1 hour and up to 6 hours, turning occasionally to cover both sides. Transfer the loin steaks to a plate, reserving the marinade.

Prepare a fire in a charcoal grill or preheat a gas grill to medium-high heat. Place the loin steaks on the grill slightly away from the direct heat and allow to cook for approximately 8 to 10 minutes, occasionally moving them (still on the same side) to prevent overcooking or charring. Flip the loin steaks and continue to cook for an additional 5 minutes or until the steak is completely cooked through and is still very light pink in the center, reaching an internal temperature of 145°F. Remove the steaks from the grill and let stand for 5 to 10 minutes before slicing.

Meanwhile, transfer the cranberry mixture to a saucepan and cook over medium-high heat to a boil. Reduce the heat to medium and cook for 3 minutes.

Serve hot, topped with the warmed cranberry mixture.

Fireball Shrimp
Fried Pepper Shrimp

To devein or not to devein, that is the question. Certainly in a recipe like this you can't really see the grit in the shrimp. You can't really taste it either, but you know it's there. I always spend the time to take it out, because who wants to eat that stuff?

Serves 4   **Prep time: 30 minutes**

Heat rating:  **(with Insanity Sauce)**

1 ¹/₂ pounds fresh or frozen medium shrimp, peeled and deveined

2 cups all-purpose flour, plus additional for dredging

¹/₄ teaspoon baking powder

1 teaspoon salt

2 fresh green jalapeño chiles, stemmed, seeded, and very finely minced

2 drops Insanity Sauce (optional)

1 teaspoon ground cayenne pepper

2 eggs, lightly beaten

¹/₂ cup water

¹/₄ cup finely chopped fresh cilantro, leaves only

Vegetable oil, for deep-frying

Lime wedges, for garnish

Cilantro sprigs, for garnish

Insanity Seafood Sauce, for serving

Rinse and drain the shrimp and pat dry. Set aside. Combine the 2 cups flour, baking powder, salt, chiles, Insanity Sauce, cayenne, eggs, water, and chopped cilantro in a bowl and mix just until smooth. Do not overmix; some lumps will remain. Set the batter aside.

Preheat the oven to 250°F and line a large baking sheet with paper towels.

Preheat 2 inches of oil in a deep skillet or deep-fryer to 365°F or until a drop of water splatters when placed in the oil. Working in small batches, dredge the shrimp lightly in a plastic bag filled with the additional flour, then drop them into the batter. Using tongs, lift the shrimp out of the batter, allowing the excess batter to drip away prior to placing the shrimp in the oil. While frying, move the shrimp gently with a spatula so that they do not stick to the bottom of the pan. Do not overcrowd the pan, as this will cool the oil, slow the cooking, and cause the shrimp to absorb too much oil. Cook, turning occasionally, until the shrimp are golden brown and firm, about 2 minutes. Using a slotted spoon, transfer the shrimp to the paper towel–lined baking sheet to drain. (The shrimp may be made 15 minutes ahead of serving and kept warm in the preheated oven.)

To serve the shrimp, place 4 to 6 of the shrimp on each plate and garnish with lime wedges and cilantro sprigs. Serve with Insanity Seafood Sauce and no other!

The Sweet and the Crusty
Fennel and Sweet Onion–Crusted Pork Tenderloin

The title doesn't describe your marriage, but a wonderful dish that will tantalize your taste buds. Serve with grilled vegetables and Spuds and Suds (page 49).

Serves 4   Prep time: 45 minutes

Heat rating:  **(with Insanity Sauce)**

1 (2-pound) boneless pork tenderloin
2 teaspoons salt
1/2 teaspoon freshly ground black pepper
1 teaspoon ground cayenne pepper
2 tablespoons fennel seeds
1/2 teaspoon garlic powder
3 tablespoons vegetable oil
1 sweet onion (such as Walla Walla or Vidalia), peeled and very thinly sliced

1 fresh habanero chile, stemmed, seeded, and coarsely chopped
2 fresh jalapeño chiles, stemmed, seeded, and coarsely chopped
2 cups apple cider
1/4 cup apple cider vinegar
2 drops Insanity Sauce (optional)

Preheat the oven to 350°F. Generously coat the outside of the tenderloin with the salt, black and cayenne peppers, fennel, and garlic. Cut the meat into 4 equal portions, across the grain of the tenderloin, and generously coat the cut ends with salt and pepper. Reserve.

Heat the oil in a large, ovenproof sauté pan over medium heat. Sauté the onion and chiles in the oil until lightly cooked, about 1 minute. Move the onions and chiles to the sides of the pan and place the tenderloin portions, cut sides down, in the center of the pan. Sear on each side, about 2 minutes. Place the pan with the steaks, onions, and chiles into the center of the oven and bake to a minimum internal temperature of 165°F. Remove from the oven and transfer the steaks from the pan to a heated platter and cover.

Carefully handling the hot pan from the oven, deglaze the pan juices by adding the cider, vinegar, and Insanity Sauce to the pan and gently stirring over medium heat. Continue to cook the cider mixture until it is reduced by half and has a syrupy consistency, about 10 minutes. Season with salt and pepper, if necessary.

Serve the tenderloin steaks hot, with the onions, chiles, and sauce spooned over the top.

Since most of the capsaicin, and therefore the heat, is located in the ribs and seeds of a chile, removing them is called "castrating" a chile. In Mexico, they call them "capones," which also refers to neutered animals.

Another Stinkin' Crab Dish
Chile Crab Cakes with Garlic-Cilantro Sauce

My only regret is that the crabs can't be alive to enjoy this dish.

Serves 4   **Prep time: 2 hours, plus refrigeration time**

Heat rating: 🌶 🌶 🌶 🌶

2 pounds fresh cooked, canned, or frozen crabmeat, coarsely chopped

2 eggs, lightly mixed

2 cups fresh bread crumbs

2 fresh green jalapeño chiles, stemmed, seeded, and finely diced

2 teaspoons salt

$^1/_2$ teaspoon freshly ground black pepper

2 tablespoons vegetable oil, plus additional as needed

1 $^1/_2$ cups Garlic-Cilantro Sauce (recipe follows)

Cilantro leaves, for garnish

Lime wedges, for garnish

🌶 In a large bowl, combine the crabmeat, eggs, bread crumbs, chiles, salt, and pepper and mix well. Form the mixture into patties 3/4 inch thick and 3 inches in diameter. Refrigerate for about 1 hour, until cooled through.

Preheat the oven to 250°F and line a baking sheet with paper towels. Heat the 2 tablespoons of oil in a sauté pan over medium heat and cook the patties, a few at a time, until golden brown on both sides. When cooked, transfer to the prepared baking sheet to drain. Add additional oil to the pan as needed to keep the cakes from sticking. (The cakes may be made 20 minutes ahead of serving and kept warm in a 250°F oven.) For each serving, place 2 crab cakes on a plate. Stir the Garlic-Cilantro Sauce and drizzle it over each serving. Garnish with the cilantro and lime wedges.

GARLIC-CILANTRO SAUCE

Makes 1 ¹/₂ cups   **Prep time: 20 minutes, plus roasting time**

Heating rating:

1 head elephant garlic
2 tablespoons olive oil
Salt and freshly ground black pepper
1 bunch cilantro, leaves only

Juice and grated zest of 2 limes
1 fresh green jalapeño chile, stemmed,
   seeded, and coarsely chopped
¹/₂ cup plain nonfat yogurt

Preheat the oven to 350°F. Cut off the top third of the head of garlic—do not peel the cloves. Place the garlic in a small roasting pan and pour the olive oil over the top of the cloves until well coated. Lightly sprinkle the garlic with salt and pepper. Place the garlic in the oven and roast until dark golden brown and soft, 45 minutes to 1 hour. Remove and cool.

Gently press the bottom of the garlic cloves until the soft flesh pops from the husks; remove the flesh and discard the husks. Combine the garlic, cilantro, lime juice and zest, and chile in a blender and process until smooth. Pour into a bowl and stir in the yogurt. Refrigerate for 1 to 2 hours before using.

A Fishy Caper
Swordfish with Caper-Chile Sauce

This will be one of the best "jobs" that you ever masterminded—cooking jobs, that is! Stir-fried vegetables, steamed rice, or even mixed salad greens would be great accompaniments to this dish.

Serves 4   **Prep time: 30 minutes**

Heat rating:

CAPER-CHILE SAUCE
1/4 cup capers with brine
4 fresh green jalapeño chiles, stemmed, seeded, and finely chopped
2 tablespoons Roasted Chile Oil (page 33)
1 teaspoon Garlic-Chile Sauce or sriracha sauce
1 tablespoon soy sauce

Juice of 1 lemon
2 teaspoons salt
1/2 teaspoon freshly ground black pepper

4 (8-ounce) fresh swordfish fillets, 1/2 to 3/4 inch thick
1 cup Roasted Chile Oil (page 33)
4 sprigs cilantro, leaves only, for garnish

To prepare the sauce, in a small saucepan over medium heat combine all of the ingredients and cook until slightly reduced, 3 to 4 minutes. Crush the capers lightly with a spoon as the sauce heats. Adjust the seasoning to taste.

Prepare a fire in a charcoal grill or preheat a gas grill to medium-high heat. Rub the grill with a light coating of oil. Prepare the fillets by rinsing them and making sure that all of the bones have been removed and that no skin is left on the edges. Pat the fillets dry and set aside.

Rub the swordfish fillets with the chile oil on both sides and place on the grill. Grill for 6 minutes, turn with a spatula, and grill the opposite side for 6 minutes longer, or until the fish is firm and opaque.

Serve one fillet per person, topped with the caper-chile sauce and garnished with cilantro.

You may know that capers are flower buds, usually found growing in the Mediterranean. The pungent buds are dried and pickled in brine. Do you know what nonpareil capers are? "Nonpareil" in French means "without equal." These capers are small, mostly French buds that may be the best available.

Frightened Ravioli
Stuffed Ravioli with Spicy Pasta Sauce

Although I tend to use ravioli as a way to get my two-year-old to eat veggies (stuffed inside), they are an amazingly versatile food. In this recipe their demure exterior belies an incendiary filling that will render you speechless with both pleasure and pain.

Serves 4   **Prep time: 35 minutes**

Heat rating:

8 ounces ricotta cheese, softened
4 fresh red jalapeño chiles, stemmed, seeded, and finely chopped
2 teaspoons salt
1 teaspoon freshly ground black pepper
1/2 teaspoon ground cayenne pepper
8 ounces fresh ravioli pasta dough
2 eggs, lightly beaten

SAUCE
6 cloves garlic, finely chopped
2 tablespoons olive oil

1 teaspoon crushed red pepper flakes, plus additional for garnish
1 cup tomato sauce
1/4 cup stemmed chopped fresh parsley, plus additional for garnish
2 tablespoons dried oregano
1 teaspoon ground cayenne pepper
2 teaspoons salt
1/2 teaspoon freshly ground black pepper

Freshly grated Parmesan cheese, for serving (optional)

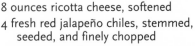 To prepare the raviolis, combine the ricotta cheese, chiles, salt, peppers, and cayenne in a small bowl and mix thoroughly. Place the pasta dough on a lightly floured work area. Roll the dough lightly with a rolling pin to achieve a uniform thickness of 1/8 inch. Cut in half.

Place a heaping tablespoonful of the ricotta mixture every 3 inches on one layer of the ravioli dough (this will be the bottom of the ravioli). Continue dropping filling onto the dough, spacing apart, until you have a total of 16 on the bottom sheet. Brush around the filling areas with the beaten egg, using a pastry brush. Place the other dough layer over the top of the filling and gently press the dough together right around the filling spots. Press to remove any trapped air that may be present. Cut around the filling areas using a cookie cutter or glass, firmly pressing through the dough layers. Set aside the finished raviolis.

To prepare the sauce, lightly sauté the garlic in the olive oil until light colored but not browned. To the garlic, add the 1 teaspoon pepper flakes, tomato sauce, parsley, oregano, cayenne, salt, and pepper and heat through, stirring occasionally, over low heat. Meanwhile, plunge the raviolis into a separate pot of boiling water for 1 minute and carefully remove using a slotted spoon. Add the pasta to the sauce at this point and finish cooking together, 3 to 4 minutes.

Serve 4 raviolis per person on a heated plate, topped with additional sauce. Garnish with parsley and additional dried chile flakes. Sprinkle with Parmesan cheese.

Catch the Tiger by the Tail
Prawns with Nuoc Cham Chile Glaze

The truth be told, we Americans call any large shrimp a prawn. Although technically they are not the same, feel free to use any large shrimp in this delicious dish.

Serves 4   **Prep time: 30 minutes, plus refrigeration time**

Heat rating:

16 large fresh prawns (about 1 pound), peeled and deveined
¹/₂ cup canola oil
¹/₂ cup rice wine vinegar
2 tablespoons toasted sesame seeds
2 teaspoons salt
¹/₂ teaspoon freshly ground black pepper
¹/₄ cup finely chopped fresh cilantro, leaves only

¹/₂ cup finely minced red onion
2 fresh green jalapeño chiles, stemmed, seeded, and very finely minced
1 cup Nuoc Cham Chile Glaze (recipe follows)
Lime wedges, for garnish
Cilantro sprigs, for garnish
Cooked rice, for serving

Rinse and drain the prawns and pat dry. Set aside. In a small bowl combine the oil, vinegar, sesame seeds, salt, pepper, chopped cilantro, onion, and chiles and mix until combined. Place the prawns in a flat dish in one layer, pour the vinaigrette over them, and cover. Marinate the prawns in the refrigerator for a minimum of 1 hour and up to 4 hours.

Prepare a fire in a charcoal grill or preheat a gas grill to medium-high heat. Remove the prawns from the vinaigrette. Place the prawns on wooden skewers if desired and grill them until crisp-tender and bright pink in color, 6 to 8 minutes. Remove the prawns and keep warm.

To serve, place 4 prawns per person onto plates and drizzle with the Nuoc Cham Chile Glaze. Surround the shrimp with the lime wedges, cilantro, and a generous scoop of cooked rice.

NUOC CHAM CHILE GLAZE

Makes ¹/₂ cup   **Prep time: 10 minutes**

Heat rating:

1 clove garlic, finely minced
1 small fresh red Thai chile, stemmed,
    seeded, and very finely minced
3 tablespoons nuoc nam (fish sauce)

Juice of 1 lime
1 teaspoon rice wine vinegar
2 tablespoons water
4 drops Garlic-Chile Sauce or sriracha sauce

To prepare the sauce, combine all of the ingredients in a small bowl, adding additional water to the mixture to thin out the sauce, if desired. Cover and refrigerate for at least 20 minutes and up to 2 hours. Bring to room temperature before serving. This is a strong sauce, so use cautiously!

Baby Bib Ribs
Applewood-Smoked Pork Ribs with Red Chile Glaze

This dish is more fun if you make a real mess when you eat it. Break out the bibs—you'll need them! Applewood chips, which add a nice, smoky flavor to the ribs, are available at most home barbecue centers. Serve the ribs with red beans and the vegetable of your choice.

Serves 4   **Prep time: 40 minutes**

Heat rating:

6 pounds pork baby back ribs
1 yellow onion, coarsely chopped
4 fresh green jalapeño chiles, stemmed,
    seeded, and coarsely chopped
12 black peppercorns

1 bay leaf
1 tablespoon cumin seeds
Applewood chips
4 cups Red Chile Glaze (recipe follows)

Prepare the ribs by removing the thin, white, skinlike membrane on the inside of the rib surface, if still present (or have your butcher do it for you). Make small slashes, using the point of a very sharp knife, between the ribs (either side is okay) without cutting all the way through. Set aside.

Combine the onion, chiles, peppercorns, bay leaf, and cumin in a deep stock pot and add water to fill half full. Bring to a boil over medium heat. When the water first reaches a boil, add the ribs. Lower the heat and simmer for 10 to 15 minutes, depending upon the rib size, or until the ribs are soft and cooked halfway through. Transfer the ribs to a plate, discarding the stock.

Preheat a grill to medium-high temperature and prepare the wood chips according to the manufacturer's instructions. Place the wood chips on the fire prior to grilling the ribs. Place the ribs on the grill and liberally baste with 2 cups of the Red Chile Glaze. Continue to grill for 8 to 10 minutes per side or until the ribs are very soft and flexible. Remove from the heat.

While the grill is the best method to use for preparing the ribs, the oven may also be used to bake the ribs. However, the applewood chips should not be used in the oven! To bake the ribs, preheat the oven to 375°F, place the ribs in an ovenproof baking pan, and liberally baste with 1 1/2 cups of the Red Chile Glaze. Place the pan in the center of the oven. Bake for a total of 25 to 30 minutes, turning the ribs over halfway through the baking process and basting with an additional 1 cup of glaze.

Serve accompanied by the remaining 1 cup of glaze.

RED CHILE GLAZE

Makes 4 cups   **Prep time: 20 minutes**

Heat rating:

2 cups pineapple juice
1/4 cup cornstarch
1 1/2 cups firmly packed brown sugar
2 teaspoons salt

1 1/2 cups rice wine vinegar
1/4 cup ketchup
4 fresh red serrano chiles, roasted,
    peeled, stemmed, and finely chopped

In a saucepan, whisk the pineapple juice and cornstarch until smooth. Add the brown sugar, salt, vinegar, ketchup, and chile flesh and cook over medium-high heat, stirring occasionally, until the mixture thickens. If the glaze gets too thick, just add a little water.

You may want to add more vinegar or juice depending on how sweet or sour you like things. The glaze will keep, covered, in the refrigerator for up to a week.

When you buy fresh chiles, go for the ones with rich, deep and vivid colors and firm flesh. Don't purchase any with soft spots or wrinkled and shriveled skin. That's a sign that they are probably a little older, just like people with the same qualities.

Za Smoke
Smoked Chile Pizzas

Pizza, we all know, is an Italian import, but did you know that it is supposedly based upon Egyptian flat bread? The sauce on this pizza is a smoky, tomatoey slice of heaven.

Serves 4   **Prep time: 50 minutes**

Heat rating:

4 prepared individual 8-inch pizza crusts, fresh or frozen
3 dried chipotle chiles
Boiling water, for soaking
1/2 cup olive oil
2 tablespoons finely minced garlic
1/4 teaspoon crushed red pepper flakes
1 (12-ounce) can chopped tomatoes
1/2 cup soft bread crumbs

1 teaspoon dried New Mexico chile powder
1 tablespoon tomato paste
2 teaspoons red wine vinegar
2 teaspoons salt
1/2 teaspoon freshly ground black pepper
Pizza toppings, such as cheese, pre-cooked meats, or vegetables
Cilantro leaves, for garnish

 Preheat the oven to 375°F. Defrost the prepared crusts, if using frozen. Soak the dried chiles in boiling water to cover until soft, about 10 minutes.

In a sauté pan, heat 2 tablespoons of the oil over medium heat, but do not allow it to smoke. Sauté the garlic, red pepper flakes, tomatoes, and bread crumbs for 3 minutes. Add the chile powder and sauté an additional 2 minutes.

Drain and carefully stem and seed the chiles and coarsely chop. Transfer the chiles and the sautéed tomato mixture to a food processor and add the tomato paste and vinegar. Process until smooth, adding the remaining 6 tablespoons of oil as the processor is running. Season with the salt and pepper.

Apply a liberal coating of the tomato-chile paste to the prepared crusts, and top with your choice of toppings. Bake in the center of the preheated oven until the top is golden brown and bubbly, 15 to 20 minutes. Cool slightly and serve, cut into wedges and garnished with cilantro leaves.

Chile and the Beast
Beef Tenderloin with Sautéed Chiles

Because there's no way that Beauty hangs out with that nasty Beast. I highly recommend getting one of those butcher charts showing which cut of meat is which; it's great to know where your food comes from. Tenderloins are from the middle of the back and are actually the source of filet mignon. They are tender and delicious. Serve with grilled vegetables and Spuds and Suds (page 49).

Serves: 8   **Prep time: 35 minutes**

Heat rating:

1 (4-pound) beef tenderloin
2 teaspoons salt
1/2 teaspoon freshly ground black pepper
1 teaspoon ground cayenne pepper
3 tablespoons vegetable oil
2 fresh Anaheim chiles, stemmed, seeded, and coarsely chopped

1 fresh habanero chile, stemmed, seeded, and coarsely chopped
2 fresh jalapeño chiles, stemmed, seeded, and coarsely chopped
1 ripe tomato, peeled, seeded, and coarsely chopped
2 tablespoons cold butter

Preheat the oven to 400°F.

Generously coat the outside of the tenderloin with the salt, pepper, and cayenne. Cut the meat into 8 equal portions, across the grain of the tenderloin, and generously coat the cut ends with salt and pepper as well. Set aside.

Heat the oil in a large, ovenproof pan over medium heat. Sauté the chiles and tomato in the oil until lightly cooked, about 1 minute. Move the chiles and tomato to the sides of the pan and place the cuts of tenderloin in the center of the pan. Sear on each side for 1 to 2 minutes, without moving the tenderloin between turning. Remove from the heat. Add the butter, in small pieces, to the pan, and swirl the butter around to combine. Place the pan with the steaks and chiles in the center of the oven. Bake to the desired degree of doneness or until the steaks feel medium-firm to the touch, 6 to 8 minutes.

Serve hot with the chiles and tomato spooned over the top.

We refer to "ovenproof" pans as those which are able to be used both on top of the stove and in the oven. Pans with plastic handles or any parts that could burn or melt are not advisable. A good rule of thumb for some of the recipes that call for ovenproof pans is to use a pan with all-metal construction, including the handle, rivets, and lid.

Estuary Enchiladas
Shrimp Enchiladas with Piquant Pesto

Now I'm not really sure what an estuary is. I know that it is a body of water and that the word sounds like mortuary. Luckily, I don't have to know what the word means to know that these are good enchiladas, and I love enchiladas. Whether you like lamb, beef, chicken, fish, or pork, or are a vegetarian, there is a great enchilada for you. If you are a fruitarian (people who eat only fruit), then you have my deepest sympathies. Serve these shrimp-filled enchiladas with refried beans and Spanish rice.

Serves 4   Prep time: 50 minutes

Heat rating:

2 tablespoons plus ¹/₄ cup olive oil
4 shallots, diced
2 tomatoes, diced
32 medium shrimp (about 1 pound), peeled and deveined
¹/₄ cup tequila
³/₄ teaspoon salt

2 bunches cilantro, leaves only
3 fresh serrano chiles
6 cloves garlic
Juice of 1 lime
8 medium flour tortillas
1 cup grated pepper Jack cheese
4 cherry tomatoes, halved

Preheat the oven to 400°F.

Heat the 2 tablespoons olive oil in a skillet over moderate heat. Add half of the diced shallots and all of the diced tomatoes. Cook 3 minutes, stirring occasionally. Add the shrimp and cook another 3 minutes, or until the shrimp turn pink. Add the tequila and salt and cook for 1 to 2 minutes. Remove from the heat.

In a food processor or blender, combine the cilantro, chiles, garlic, the remaining diced shallots, and the lime juice. While the processor is running, carefully add the ¹/₄ cup olive oil in a stream until the pesto is thick and well blended.

To assemble the enchiladas, spread about 1 tablespoon pesto over one side of a tortilla. Fill the dry side of the tortilla with some of the shrimp mixture, putting 4 shrimp in each enchilada. Roll up the enchilada so the pesto side is on the outside (this will be a messy process). Place it seam side down in a 9 by 13-inch baking dish. Continue assembling the enchiladas until all of the shrimp and tortillas are used. If there is any remaining pesto, pour it over the enchiladas in the baking dish.

Sprinkle the top of the enchiladas with the cheese. Top each with 2 cherry tomato halves. Bake for 10 to 15 minutes, or until the cheese is melted.

Maniacal Mahi Mahi
Mahi Mahi with Mango Salsa

Have you ever gone swimming in the ocean in the middle of winter? You'd have to be nuts. That is what these fish do, the little maniacs. It is no wonder they get caught; their brains are probably so frozen they think the hook is a yummy little Snickers bar. This preparation of the fish is light, healthy, and delectable. Enjoy. Serve with jasmine rice cooked in equal parts coconut milk and water and garnished with chopped and toasted macadamia nuts.

Serves 4 **Prep time: 25 minutes**

Heat rating:

MANGO SALSA
2 mangos
2 oranges, such as Valencia
Juice of 1 lime
$^1/_4$ cup chopped fresh mint
$^1/_4$ cup diced red onion
2 teaspoons salt

2 fresh habanero chiles, seeded and minced

1 teaspoon salt
1 teaspoon ground cayenne pepper
2 teaspoons vegetable oil
4 (7-ounce) mahi mahi fillets

Preheat the broiler.

To prepare the salsa, peel and pit the mangos and cut into $^1/_2$-inch cubes. Peel and section the oranges, cutting away all white pith. Chop each orange section into 3 pieces. Combine the mangos, oranges, lime juice, mint, onion, salt, and chiles in a bowl and mix well. Set aside.

Sprinkle the salt, cayenne pepper, and oil over the fish. Rub the oil and seasonings into both sides of the fillets. Place on an oiled broiler pan and broil the fish for 4 to 5 minutes per side, until flaky and cooked through.

Transfer the fillets to serving plates and spoon some of the mango salsa over each piece of fish. Serve immediately.

Smell can also be a good way to determine the flavor of a chile, since the nose can pick up about ten thousand distinct aromas.

Daring Dairy Cow
Blue Cheese–Stuffed Filet Mignon

This is one of those dishes that should be served in a fine steak house. When you start with filet mignon and a good blue cheese, you can do no wrong. You might even want to make a mild version and share with those riffraff non–chile eaters in your house. Be aware that blue cheese should not be 100 percent blue. If it is, then you might want to scrape off the outside a little bit.

Serves 4   **Prep time: 50 minutes**

Heat rating:

4 fresh green jalapeño chiles, stemmed, seeded, and finely minced

8 ounces soft blue cheese, such as Danish Blue or Cambozola

1 teaspoon ground cayenne pepper

2 teaspoons salt

4 sprigs cilantro, leaves only, finely chopped

4 (8-ounce) filet mignon steaks, cut 3 inches thick

1 teaspoon kosher salt

1/2 teaspoon freshly ground black pepper

Insanity Steak Sauce or other steak sauce, for serving

Preheat the oven to 350°F or a gas grill to medium-high heat.

Prepare the filling by combining the chiles, cheese, cayenne, and salt in a small bowl. Add the cilantro and mix until homogenous.

Place a filet on its edge on a secure cutting board and, using a small, very sharp knife, cut down into the filet approximately halfway through. Leaving the filet in place, move the knife back and forth, from side to side, to open a small pocket in the center of the filet. Repeat with each filet. Fill each steak pocket with one-fourth of the cheese mixture.

If using the oven, preheat an ovenproof sauté pan over medium-high heat and sear the cut sides (not the filled sides) of each filet until dark brown on each side. Place the filets, still in the pan, in the center of the oven and bake until the filets reach the desired degree of doneness, about 8 minutes for medium-rare.

If using a grill, cook the filets on each side for approximately 8 to 10 minutes or until the filets reach the desired degree of doneness.

Season with the salt and pepper and serve topped with Insanity Steak Sauce.

Mac Attack
Mac and Cheese

Be careful about bringing this one to a block party—you wouldn't want your neighbors to trim your hedges into a skull and crossbones during the night.

Serves 6   **Prep time: 1 hour**

Heat rating: (with Insanity Sauce)

1 pound cavatappi pasta (or other macaroni, even elbow)

1/4 cup plus 1 1/2 tablespoons unsalted butter

1/4 cup all-purpose flour

4 cups whole milk

1 fresh jalapeño chile, stemmed, seeded, and minced

1 fresh red Fresno chile, stemmed, seeded, and minced

1 teaspoon dry mustard powder

1/4 teaspoon ground cayenne pepper

1 to 2 drops Insanity Sauce (optional)

Salt and freshly ground black pepper

3 cups grated Vermont or New York sharp Cheddar cheese

1 1/4 cups freshly grated Parmesan cheese (don't use the canned powdered kind; I think that stuff might actually be sawdust, but I'm not sure)

1 cup bread crumbs

Preheat the oven to 350°F. Grease a 4-quart baking dish with butter.

Cook the pasta in a large pot of boiling salted water until al dente, 7 or 8 minutes. (Be sure not to overcook it, since it will cook more when you bake it later.) Drain and rinse with cold water to stop the cooking. Drain again and set aside.

In a saucepan, melt the 1/4 cup butter over medium-low heat. Add the flour and whisk for 3 or 4 minutes. Continue mixing while adding the milk, and bring to a boil. Reduce the heat to a simmer and add the chiles, mustard, cayenne, Insanity Sauce (be careful!), and salt and pepper to taste. Gently simmer the sauce for a few minutes, stirring occasionally, until thick and the flavors are combined.

In a large bowl, mix together the pasta, sauce, Cheddar, and 1 cup of the Parmesan. Transfer to the prepared baking dish.

In a small bowl, mix the bread crumbs and the remaining 1/4 cup Parmesan; spread evenly over the pasta. Dot the top of the bread crumbs with the 1 1/2 tablespoons butter.

Bake for 25 minutes or until you can't stand to see its beautiful, bubbling self trapped in that oven any longer! Cool just a little bit before serving, just to give your tongue a fighting chance against the Insanity Sauce.

Pit Bull on a Stick
Corn Dogs

Does your dog bite? This dog may be corny, but he has a sharp bite.

Serves 6   **Prep time: 1 hour**

Heat rating:

6 hot dogs, whatever brand you like
6 Popsicle sticks
$^1/_3$ cup cornmeal
$^1/_2$ teaspoon dry mustard powder
1 teaspoon Insanity Spice or dried habanero chile flakes
2 teaspoons ground cayenne pepper
$^1/_4$ teaspoon finely ground white pepper

$^1/_2$ teaspoon salt
$^1/_2$ cup all-purpose flour
1 teaspoon baking powder
1 tablespoon solid vegetable shortening
1 large egg
$^1/_2$ cup milk
Vegetable oil, for deep-frying

 Line a baking sheet with paper towels. Insert sticks into the end of each hot dog, making a handle, and place on the baking sheet.

In a large bowl, mix together the cornmeal, mustard, Insanity Spice, cayenne, white pepper, salt, flour, and baking powder. In a small bowl, beat the egg and milk together, and pour into the dry mixture. Stir with a wooden spoon until all lumps have disappeared.

In a tall saucepan add enough oil to vertically submerge one hot dog (you are going to fry them two at a time). Heat the oil to 350°F.

Pour the batter into a glass tall enough to totally submerge a hot dog. One at a time, dip two hot dogs into the batter, then submerge them in the hot oil. (Doing them two at a time will ensure an even oil temperature and a consistent finished product.) You should be able to do this with your hands, holding the sticks until the batter becomes golden brown, about 5 minutes, being extra careful not to touch the hot oil. You can also drop the dogs in whole and fish them out by grabbing the sticks with a pair of tongs. Transfer to the prepared baking sheet to drain. Repeat until all 6 are finished.

Drive a Steak through My Taco
Grilled Steak Tacos with Chiles and Peppers

This one is a particular favorite of those who choose to mount horns on the front of their Cadillacs. Hey, don't knock it—what other kind of car do you think chileheads drive? Along with the warm tortillas, serve with chopped tomatoes, grilled onions, lettuce, guacamole, and sour cream for a little fajita action!

Serves 2, but can easily be multiplied for the number of diners

Prep time: 45 minutes or less

Heat rating: **(with Insanity Sauce)**

8 ounces beef flank steak
Salt and freshly ground black pepper
2 tablespoons canola oil
1 red onion, thinly sliced
1 red bell pepper, stemmed, seeded, and sliced in ¹/₄-inch strips
1 yellow bell pepper, stemmed, seeded, and sliced in ¹/₄-inch strips
1 fresh red Fresno chile, stemmed, seeded, and minced

2 fresh green serrano chiles, stemmed, seeded, and minced
3 to 4 drops Insanity Sauce (optional)
¹/₂ teaspoon ground cumin
¹/₂ teaspoon ground cayenne pepper
¹/₂ teaspoon ground ancho chile
2 tablespoons minced fresh cilantro
Corn tortillas, for serving

Prepare a fire in a charcoal grill or preheat a gas grill to medium heat. Lightly season the steak with salt and pepper. Grill, turning once, until cooked to medium, about 6 to 8 minutes, or to desired doneness. Remove from the grill to a platter and allow to rest 5 to 10 minutes. Slice ¹/₃ inch thick and set aside.

Heat the oil in a large skillet over medium heat. Add the onion and bell peppers and cook until tender, about 10 minutes. Add the sliced steak, chiles, Insanity Sauce, cumin, cayenne, ground ancho, and salt and pepper to taste. Warm through, but don't cook it too much, or the meat will overcook and become tough. You might have to add a tablespoon or two of water to keep the mixture moist. Remove from the heat, transfer to a bowl and sprinkle the cilantro over the top. Serve with warm tortillas.

Meat and fish should never be left out long enough that its temperature rises above 40°F, so this tip might help those who keep lots of stuff in the freezer. Whenever possible, thaw meats and fish in the refrigerator for 24 to 48 hours before using. If this isn't possible, fish and poultry can be thawed by wrapping tightly in plastic and placing under *cold,* slowly running water. You can also thaw in your microwave, but *never* thaw meats and fish by leaving them out on the counter. Bacteria love to grow at room temperature, and not even Insanity Sauce can kill the little critters that might find your dinner before you do!

Terrifying Tubes
Penne all'Arrabbiata

This is a classic Polish dish and should be served with kielbasa and borsht. It should be paired with a 1997 Manishevitz or a 1999 Mad Dog. If you believe that, then call me right away about a lucrative investment in Nigeria. This is actually a common Italian dish that you see quite a bit on American menus. *Buon gusto.*

Serves 4   Prep time: 45 minutes

Heat rating: 🌶 🌶 🌶 🌶 🌶 🌶 **(with Insanity Sauce)**

1 tablespoon olive oil
2 shallots, finely chopped
2 cloves garlic, minced
6 ounces pancetta, diced
1 (28-ounce) can puréed tomatoes
1 teaspoon ground chile powder

3 dried chiles de árbol, stemmed and
    ground in a mortar and pestle
1 to 2 drops Insanity Sauce (optional)
1 pound dried penne pasta
1 cup grated Parmesan cheese

Heat a large sauté pan over medium heat and add the oil. Add the shallots, then the garlic, and sauté until soft. Add the pancetta and sauté until brown, about 3 minutes. Stir in the tomatoes, chile powder, ground chiles, and Insanity Sauce and cook for about 5 minutes, until the flavors combine. Keep warm.

Cook the pasta in a large pot of boiling water until al dente, about 10 minutes. Drain and transfer to a large bowl. Stir in the tomato sauce and 1/2 cup of the cheese. Serve with the remaining cheese in a bowl for sprinkling.

For the fans of super-hot sauces out there in the world, this is how the extracts like some of the ones we use are made. You can perform a similar process at home with a very strong alcohol. The basic procedure for the manufacture of oleoresin is as follows: Chiles are ground into tiny particles. The particles are blasted with industrial solvents. The solvents are distilled off and the remaining super-hot compound is mixed in oil and packaged.

The Colonel's Evil Twin Brother's Chicken
Asian Style—Fried Chicken with Mustard-Chile Sauce

This is Asian-style fried chicken, without all the crust, but with tons of flavor.

Serves 6 to 8   **Prep time: 30 minutes, plus marinating time**

Heat rating: **(with Insanity Sauce)**

MARINADE
1 tablespoon curry powder

1 tablespoon ground cayenne pepper

1 teaspoon Insanity Spice or dried habanero chile flakes

2 to 4 drops Insanity Sauce (optional)

2 tablespoons soy sauce

2 tablespoons freshly squeezed lemon juice

2 tablespoons freshly squeezed lime juice

2 teaspoons salt

2 teaspoons sugar

1 (3-pound) frying chicken, rinsed and cut into serving pieces

MUSTARD-CHILE SAUCE
$1/2$ cup Worcestershire sauce

1 teaspoon dried mustard powder

3 fresh Thai chiles or red serrano chiles, stemmed, seeded, and minced

$1/4$ to $1/2$ teaspoon salt

$1/4$ teaspoon freshly ground black pepper

Canola oil, for deep-frying

In a bowl, mix together all of the marinade ingredients. Transfer to a large plastic zipper bag, along with the chicken. Turn to coat the chicken. Marinate in the refrigerator for 4 hours or overnight, turning occasionally.

In a small glass jar, mix together all of the ingredients for the sauce, being careful not to go overboard with the salt since there's salt in the marinade. Make sure the mustard is well blended. Let sit in the glass jar for 1 hour, or, if making in advance, in the refrigerator for up to 24 hours. Warm the sauce up a little before serving. (You can multiply this sauce recipe however you'd like, but just make sure the mustard gets well blended.)

Preheat the oven to 250°F and line a large baking sheet with paper towels.

Heat 6 to 8 inches of oil in a deep heavy pot or deep-fryer to about 350°F. Drain the marinade from the chicken and carefully deep-fry the chicken in small batches. Transfer to the prepared baking sheet to drain, then transfer again to an ovenproof dish and place in the oven to keep warm. Serve hot with the warm sauce on the side.

Hot Cha Cha Chops
Roasted Lamb Chops with Scotch Bonnets and Sage

After a few bites of this dish, your mouth won't know if it is supposed to mambo or merengue, but it will be dancing. This is a basic Mediterranean-Caribbean dish. Once you get past the culture shock and learn to dance, it is a delicious dish to serve most any time. Try it with couscous or rice and a Greek salad.

Serves 6   **Prep time: 1 hour**

Heat rating:

MARINADE
1/2 cup freshly squeezed lemon juice
1 tablespoon minced garlic
1/4 cup chopped fresh mint leaves
2 fresh Scotch bonnet chiles, stemmed, seeded, and minced

12 (4- to 5-ounce) lamb chops, each 1 inch thick

RUB
2 tablespoons salt
1 tablespoon dried ground sage
1 1/2 teaspoons Insanity Spice or dried habanero chile flakes
1/2 teaspoon chopped lemon zest

6 tablespoons canola oil

 Preheat the oven to 450°F.

In a small bowl, mix together the marinade ingredients. Place the chops in a large container and pour the marinade over them. Turn to coat. Cover with plastic wrap and refrigerate for 20 minutes or so.

Mix together all of the rub ingredients in a small bowl and pour onto a large plate. One at a time, remove the chops from the marinade and dip into the rub mixture, coating each side.

In a large skillet, heat 2 tablespoons of the oil and brown each side of the chops, 4 at a time, 1 to 2 minutes on each side, adding 2 tablespoons of the oil before each batch. Transfer the chops to a baking pan and roast all of them in the oven until medium-rare, about 10 to 12 minutes.

Kung Fu Chicken
Cashew-Chicken Stir-Fry

It would seem that Kung Fu Crane might be a more appropriate title, but finding crane in a local market is really tough. Not to mention that crane tends to be a tad large for most woks or sauté pans. Chicken just seems more practical. If it is a little too mundane for you, burn some incense while you cook this. Either way, this recipe is an unusual and delicious twist on stir-fried chicken.

Serves 4   **Prep time: 45 minutes or less**

Heat rating:

4 tablespoons soy sauce
2 tablespoons sherry
2 tablespoons cornstarch
1 pound boneless skinless chicken breasts, cut into 3/4-inch dice
1 1/2 teaspoons sugar
2 tablespoons rice vinegar
2 teaspoons toasted sesame oil
1/3 cup water
2 tablespoons canola oil

1/2 cup cashews
1 small white onion, cut into 1/2-inch dice
2 cloves garlic, minced
2 fresh red Fresno chiles, stemmed, seeded, and minced
10 dried chiles de árbol or dried Thai chiles, broken in half and stems removed
2 green onions, white part only, cut diagonally into 1/2-inch pieces
Steamed rice, for serving

In a small bowl, whisk together 1 tablespoon each of the soy sauce, sherry, and cornstarch. Place the chicken in a shallow dish, coat with the soy sauce mixture, and marinate in the refrigerator for 20 minutes to 3 hours.

In a small bowl, mix the remaining 3 tablespoons soy sauce, 1 tablespoon sherry, 1 tablespoon corn starch, and the sugar, vinegar, sesame oil, and water.

In a large sauté pan or wok, heat 1 tablespoon of the canola oil until quite hot. Add the cashews and stir-fry until they just turn color. This won't take long, and they burn easily, so be careful. Using a slotted spoon, remove the cashews from the wok and set aside. Add the remaining tablespoon of oil and the white onions to the wok and stir-fry until the onions start to soften, about 2 minutes. Add the garlic and Fresno chiles and stir-fry for about 20 seconds, being careful not to let the garlic brown. Add the dried chiles and cook until the chiles start to release their aroma, less than a minute. Add the chicken with its marinade and stir-fry for about 2 minutes, until the chicken is still a little pink. (If you overcook the chicken here, it will be dry.) Add the soy sauce mixture and the green onions and stir-fry until the chicken is no longer pink, about 4 minutes. Add the nuts and stir until all of the ingredients are coated with the sauce. Serve hot, with steamed rice.

Balls of Fire
Meatball Soup

Goodness gracious . . . this is a spicy meat-a-ball. This soup is a great change of pace—
a case of minestrone meets monster meatballs. The soup is hearty, filling, and healthy.

Serves 4   Prep time: 55 minutes

Heat rating:

MEATBALLS

1/2 pound ground beef

2 1/2 tablespoons chopped fresh
  flat-leaf parsley

1/4 cup grated Parmesan cheese

3 fresh red Fresno chiles, stemmed,
  seeded, and minced

2 tablespoons dry bread crumbs

1 egg, beaten

3 cloves garlic, minced

1/2 teaspoon salt

1/4 teaspoon freshly ground black pepper

2 tablespoons olive oil

2 carrots, cut into 1/4-inch dice

2 onions, cut into 1/2-inch dice

2 ribs celery, cut into 1/4-inch dice

2 cloves garlic, minced

4 cups low-sodium chicken broth

2 cups water

1 cup canned crushed tomatoes in purée

1 1/2 teaspoons salt

5 fresh red serrano chiles, cut crosswise
  into 1/4-inch rounds

1 cup small dried rotini macaroni

Chopped fresh flat-leaf parsley,
  for garnish

To prepare the meatballs, in a large bowl, gently blend all of the meatball ingredients. Shape into meatballs, about the size of golf balls. Don't overwork the meatballs, as they get a little dry. Set aside.

In a soup pot, heat the oil over medium heat and add the carrots, onion, and celery and cook about 3 minutes, stirring occasionally, or until they start to soften. Then add the garlic and cook, stirring, until you can smell the garlic, about 2 minutes. Add the broth, water, tomatoes and bring to a boil. Lower the heat to a simmer, and add 1 teaspoon of the salt, the chiles, macaroni, and meatballs. Cook until the macaroni is tender and the meatballs are cooked through, about 20 minutes.

When the macaroni and meatballs are cooked, check the seasoning (it will probably need the pepper and just a little salt, but remember, the meatballs are pretty spicy). Pour the soup into bowls, and sprinkle a little of the chopped parsley on top of each serving.

Serve hot. This soup also tastes great as a reheated leftover, after the flavors have had a chance to come together during refrigeration.

Shmokin' Shrimp
Shrimp With Chipotle-Orange Glaze

This sweet, smoky treatment for shrimp is a real winner. It has a big flavor that will have them coming back for more. You can serve the shrimp over rice, in salads, with pasta, or in a sandwich.

Serves 6

Prep time: 50 minutes, plus 2 hours chilling time (the shrimp, not you)

Heat rating:

2 tablespoons olive oil
1 cup finely chopped onion
5 cloves garlic, minced
2 teaspoons ground cumin
1 teaspoon dried oregano
1 cup water
1/4 cup apple cider vinegar

2 to 3 tablespoons chopped canned chipotle chiles in adobo sauce
1 1/2 pounds jumbo shrimp, peeled and deveined
1/4 cup freshly squeezed orange juice
2 tablespoons firmly packed golden brown sugar

Heat the oil in heavy sauté pan over medium heat. Add the onion and sauté until golden, about 10 minutes. Add the garlic, cumin, and oregano; cook and stir 1 minute. Transfer the mixture to a blender. Add the 1 cup water, vinegar, and chiles to the blender; purée until smooth. Transfer half of the purée to a large bowl; cool. Add the shrimp to the bowl; toss to coat. Cover and refrigerate for 2 hours.

Pour the remaining purée into a heavy saucepan. Add the orange juice and brown sugar. Bring to a boil, decrease the heat, and simmer until the glaze is slightly thickened and reduced to 1/2 cup, about 10 minutes. Remove from the heat. Cover.

Prepare a fire in a charcoal grill or preheat a gas grill to medium heat. Remove the shrimp from the marinade and pat dry with paper towels. Place the shrimp on the grill then brush with some of the orange juice glaze. Grill the shrimp until opaque in the center, brushing occasionally with more glaze, about 2 minutes per side. Serve immediately.

Chicken à la Hash
Chicken-Chile Hash

I admit that I am not usually a big hash fan because they can be too greasy, look funky, and don't really have enough flavor. This dish definitely does not fit that description. It can be a meal by itself, and you can really take creative license with what you include. Want habanero? Add it. Chipotle? Add it. Mango? Don't even think about it. Serve with eggs and toast.

Serves 6   **Prep time: 55 minutes**

Heat rating:

4 cups chicken broth

2 whole boneless skinless chicken breasts (about 1 1/2 pounds), halved

1 1/2 pounds small red potatoes, cut into 1/2-inch cubes

1 large onion, chopped fine

1 small green bell pepper, seeded and cut into 1/4-inch dice

1 small red bell pepper, seeded and cut into 1/4-inch dice

3 cloves garlic, minced

2 tablespoons unsalted butter

1 teaspoon paprika

3/4 teaspoon ground chile powder

1/2 teaspoon freshly ground black pepper

3/4 teaspoon ground white pepper

3/4 teaspoon dried thyme, crumbled

3/4 teaspoon salt

1/2 cup chopped green onion, white part only

1/2 cup packed fresh parsley leaves, chopped

1 cup half-and-half

1 tablespoon Cool Cayenne Pepper Sauce or other Louisiana-style hot sauce

In a deep 12-inch skillet bring the broth to a boil and add the chicken breasts. Lower the heat to a simmer and poach the chicken, turning once, for 7 minutes. Remove the skillet from the heat and cool the chicken in the broth for 20 minutes. Discard the liquid and cut the chicken into 1/2-inch cubes.

In a large saucepan of boiling salted water, cook the potatoes until tender, about 5 minutes. Drain in a colander.

In a heavy 12-inch skillet cook the onion, bell peppers, and garlic in butter over moderately high heat, stirring frequently, until softened, about 3 minutes. Add the paprika, chile powder, black and white pepper, thyme, and salt and cook, stirring, 1 minute. Add the chicken, potatoes, green onion, parsley, and half-and-half and cook over moderately high heat, stirring occasionally, until the half-and-half is reduced slightly and the hash has thickened. Add hot sauce, stir, and serve.

Chicken Dijonotle
Grilled Chicken with Dijon-Chipotle Sauce

The sauce in this dish brings together an unusual combination of ingredients to make an outstanding flavor. It is essentially a sour cream–chipotle dijonaise dip. Chilled, the sauce is also great as a dipping sauce for roasted new potatoes.

Serves 6   **Prep time: 45 minutes**

Heat rating:

DIJON-CHIPOTLE SAUCE
2 egg yolks, at room temperature
2 teaspoons white wine vinegar
1 teaspoon Dijon mustard
1/4 teaspoon salt
1 1/2 cups olive oil or vegetable oil or a combination of the two

3 minced canned chipotle chiles in adobo sauce (or more, if you dare) plus 3 tablespoons of the juice
2 teaspoons freshly squeezed lemon juice
1/2 cup sour cream

6 boneless skinless chicken breast halves

To prepare the sauce, in a medium bowl, whisk together the egg yolks, vinegar, mustard, and salt. Slowly whisk in 1/2 cup of the oil, a few teaspoons at a time, and then add the remaining 1 cup of oil in a stream, beating until the mixture is emulsified. Stir in the chipotles with their juice, lemon juice, and sour cream. Chill the dipping sauce, covered, for at least 1 hour or overnight.

Prepare a fire in charcoal grill or preheat a gas grill to medium heat. Grill the chicken until cooked through (no longer pink and juices are clear), turning occasionally, about 12 minutes. Transfer chicken breasts to plates. Top with the sauce and serve.

Mr. McDonald's Secret Burger
Green Chile Cheeseburger with
Roasted Red Pepper Ketchup

If Ray Kroc was from New Mexico, we would all be eating these. Every year when we chileheads make our pilgrimage to the Fiery Foods Show in Albuquerque, I am pleasantly surprised by the roasted green chile atop most of the hamburgers. This recipe is a variation on that theme. You will never go back to a plain old burger.

Serves 4   Prep time: 1 hour

Heat rating:

GREEN CHILE SAUCE
6 fresh Anaheim chiles
1 fresh poblano chile
2 tablespoons minced white onion
2 cloves garlic, minced
3 tablespoons olive oil
1 1/2 teaspoons all-purpose flour
1/3 cup water
Salt

ROASTED RED PEPPER KETCHUP
1 (16-ounce) can diced tomatoes
1 (8-ounce) jar roasted red peppers, drained
1 cup chopped red onion

1/2 cup dry red wine
6 tablespoons golden brown sugar
2 large dried ancho chiles, stemmed, seeded, and chopped
2 tablespoons tomato paste
2 tablespoons red wine vinegar
1 tablespoon fennel seeds
2 teaspoons chopped garlic
1 1/2 teaspoons ground cumin
1 bay leaf
Salt and freshly ground black pepper

1 1/2 pounds ground beef
4 slices Cheddar or Swiss cheese
4 hamburger buns

To prepare the chile sauce, roast, peel, seed, and chop the chiles. In a heavy saucepan, cook the onion and garlic in the oil over moderately low heat, stirring, until soft, 2 to 3 minutes. Sprinkle the flour over the onion mixture and stir with a wooden spoon until well combined.

Trickle in the water, stirring constantly, and stir in the chiles. Bring the mixture to a simmer, stirring frequently. Decrease the heat to moderately low and cook the mixture, stirring, until thickened, 3 to 4 minutes. Add salt to taste.

To prepare the ketchup, combine the tomatoes with their juices, red peppers, onion, wine, sugar, chiles, tomato paste, vinegar, fennel seeds, garlic, cumin, and bay leaf in a heavy saucepan over high heat. Bring to a boil. Decrease the heat to medium and simmer until reduced to about 3 cups, about 30 minutes. Discard the bay leaf. Working in batches, purée the ketchup in a blender until smooth. Season with salt and pepper to taste. (The ketchup will keep, refrigerated and in an airtight jar, for up to 3 weeks.)

Prepare a fire in a charcoal grill or preheat a gas grill to medium heat. Divide the beef into 4 equal portions and form each into a patty. Cook the burgers to desired doneness, flipping once, 10 to 12 minutes for medium-rare. One minute before they are done, place 1 slice of the cheese on top of each burger.

Serve the burgers on the buns, topped with a 1 heaping tablespoon of the chile sauce and 1 tablespoon of the ketchup.

Pig in a Burgundy Blanket
Pork Roast with Chile Colorado (Red Sauce)

This is the sauce that your enchiladas have been waiting for. Your roasted pork will never be the same. Your grilled chicken is about to be elevated. That is, if you don't eat this up on tortilla chips first. This is an incredible sauce; brace yourself.

Serves 6   **Prep time: 1 hour**

Heat rating:  (with Total Insanity Sauce)

1 tablespoon vegetable oil
1 (2- to 3-pound) pork shoulder roast
Salt and freshly ground black pepper

SAUCE
2 dried New Mexico chiles, rinsed, stemmed, and seeded
2 dried guajillo chiles, rinsed, stemmed, and seeded
4 cups boiling water

3 tablespoons finely chopped white onion
3 cloves garlic, minced
1 1/2 teaspoons ground cumin
3/4 teaspoon dried oregano
2 tablespoons vegetable oil
1 tablespoon all-purpose flour
2 teaspoons sherry vinegar, or to taste
1 teaspoon sugar
1 tablespoon kosher salt, or to taste
Dash of Total Insanity Sauce (optional)

Preheat the oven to 325°F.

In a large, heavy skillet over medium-high heat, heat the oil. Add the roast and brown on all sides. Place the roast in a heavy roasting pan with a tight-fitting lid, or in a large baking pan that you can seal with aluminum foil. Sprinkle the roast with the salt and pepper and bake in the center of the oven for 35 to 45 minutes per pound, or until the meat reaches an internal temperature of 165°F. Remove the roast and allow to cool slightly. Slice the roast into 1/2-inch-thick slices.

Meanwhile, to prepare the sauce, heat a cast iron skillet over moderate heat. Add the chiles and toast, in batches, about 30 seconds, without burning. Transfer the chiles after toasting to a heatproof bowl and pour the water over them. Cover the bowl and soak the chiles, stirring occasionally, until softened, about 15 minutes. Drain the chiles, reserving the liquid.

Purée the chiles in a blender with three-fourths of the soaking liquid (reserve the remaining soaking liquid) until smooth. Pour the purée through a coarse sieve into a bowl, pressing on the solids. Discard the solids. Whisk the reserved soaking liquid into the strained chile mixture. Set aside.

Cook the onion, garlic, cumin, and oregano in the oil in large, heavy saucepan over moderately low heat, stirring, for 2 minutes. Add the flour and cook, stirring, for 2 minutes. Whisk in the chile purée and simmer, partially covered and whisking occasionally, until reduced to about 2 1/2 cups, 25 to 30 minutes. Add the vinegar, sugar, salt, and Total Insanity Sauce. To serve, place slices of the roast on individual serving plates, and top each with 3 tablespoons of the sauce.

The Antidote

Although I am sure that you never have eaten anything too spicy and that you can tolerate anything, I know that you may know somebody who will eat something a little too hot for them. For that person it is handy to know how to handle the situation. I have actually spent a great deal of time researching this problem over the past decade.

The part of a chile that is hot is an alkaloid compound called capsaicin, located most heavily in the veins and seeds of the chile. Since it is an alkaloid substance, I experimented with acids to counteract it. I found that fruits and fruit juices were not helpful and that drinking Clorox would have been a case in which the solution was worse than the problem.

Many people say that sugar, starches (bread), or fats are the way to cure the problem. While capsaicin is lipophilic (it likes fat lipids) and some of the items in this group will absorb and dilute the capsaicin, I have not found any of these to be an effective antidote. It is also said that dairy products can be helpful. One theory is that the milk protein casein counteracts the chiles. I tested this out and found that casein tastes really bad by itself and that dairy products did not make a big difference.

The question then is, what does help? In my exhaustive, but really unscientific studies, I have found only one factor that really helps. It is cold. If you keep the affected area really cold with ice or ice cream for fifteen minutes, that usually does the trick. I might also recommend wiping any burning spot with a clean, dry cloth to try and absorb the capsaicin before applying the ice.

If you should burn your hands while preparing chiles or handling hot sauces,

> Rub your hands with diluted bleach and a kitchen scrubber.
>
> Rub your hands with rubbing alcohol.
>
> Rub your hands with lemon juice. (Some kind of acid usually gets the capsaicin off the skin, but sometimes it just seems to irritate the skin.)

These family-type remedies might also help:

> Rub your hands with vegetable shortening.
>
> Rub salt in your belly button—we don't think this one works, but sometimes anything is worth a try.

Once the above remedies have kicked in, kick yourself for not having worn gloves in the first place. Shame on you!

Chile Guide

Although there are thousands of types of chile peppers sold and used around the world by lovers of the "fruit of the gods," their names may vary from country to country or even state to state. The heat of the chile may vary from chile to chile even from the same plant (since it's the plant's defense). This simple guide should help you to choose the proper chile for a dish, or at least come up with a close substitute.

Anaheim: With its mild heat (2) and flavor, this versatile chile cries out, "use me." Use in sauces and for mild chile rellenos (stuffed chiles), green chile sauce, meatloaf, and sandwiches. Anaheim chiles may be used as a replacement for bell peppers. When this chile is dried it is known as a "California chile," often used in red chile sauces.

Ancho chile: (chile on-ch-oh) This "wide chile" is actually a dried poblano chile which was green. It can have a bitter, grassy, tobacco-like, almost rubber-band flavor or a sweet dried red fruit flavor. This chile forms the base for many types of red chile sauces or Mexican moles. Usually a fairly mild heat rating of 3.

Caribe or **cera:** This chile is often mistaken for the yellow wax chile with similar flavors and size. It is used for salsas, relishes, and pickling as well as for cooking with legumes, stews, and soups. Heat rating of 3.

Cascabel: (cos-ah-vell) "Little rattle," this round to egg-shaped, dark red to brown chile has a very thin skin and flesh, which allows its seeds to rattle around. This chile has a nutty, woody taste and is often used in red chile sauces or broken up into small pieces and used in soups, stews, or sauces. Medium heat rating of 4.

Cayenne: This long, thin, bright red chile is one of the most commonly used chiles in the world. It is generally seen dried and in powedered form. A sprinkle will add a kick to almost any dish. Heat rating of 6.5

Chilaca: (chee-la-ka) This is a beautiful pepper with a long, hornlike twist and deep purple color that, as it ripens, turns to a deep brown. It is very common to find these chiles roasted, peeled, and torn into strips and served as a vegetable, cooked with beans, or made into salsas. It is best known in its dried form, where its smoky tobacco flavor comes out. When dried, this chile is known as a "pasilla" or "chile negro," which, to confuse you further, are also the names used for the dried poblano in some areas. Heat rating of 3.

Chile de árbol: (chile day-are-bowl) Also known as "bird's beak" or "chile of the tree," this chile is grown on tall plants referred to as trees. It's a close replacement for the cayenne and can be used in making salsas both cooked and raw when used in its fresh form, and in soups, sauces, and stews when dry. Medium-high heat rating of 7.

Chipotle: (chee-pote-lay or chip-oat-lay) See Jalapeño.

Fresno: This red, triangular-shaped chile can be found in most super-markets. Its heat is similar to the jalapeño, and, like the jalapeño, it is used in a wide array of dishes. Heat rating of 4.

Guajillo: (wah-he-yo) In its fresh form this chile is known as a "mirasol," or "looking at the sun." The dried guajillo is commonly used for its flavor in red chile sauces, and its medium heat rating (5) makes it great for chili.

Habanero: (hah-bah-ner-o) This fiery pepper is the hottest commonly found in the market, with a heat rating of 10. They can be found fresh in various stages of ripeness, from green to yellow to bright orange or red when fully mature, and maintain a shape similar to a Chinese lantern. There are also chocolate or dark habaneros, brown with a deeper, less flowery flavor. This chile is a chilehead mainstay, with its fruity flavor and powerful heat. The habenero is used mostly in southern Mexico and around the United States, whereas the Scotch bonnet, another chile at the top of the heat scale, is used in the Caribbean and in southern Florida and New York, where it is preferred by Haitian and Caribbean immigrants.

Hungarian: Also known as the "green Hungarian," this chile varies in color from a very light green to yellow to a bright red when fully ripened. This is a very mild pepper—heat rating of 2—with a thin skin. Enjoy it as a replacement for bell pepper in potato or macaroni salads and in meat-loaf or poultry stuffing.

Jalapeño: (hall-a-pen-yo) This deep green chile pepper is the most com-mon chile used in America (thank God for nachos). It can range from mildly hot to having some bite to it (a 5 rating). Green jalapeños have a light, fresh flavor, which makes them wonderful in dishes where just hot accent is needed. The red jalapeño has been allowed to ripen on the vine and is a deep bright red. This chile is a little sweeter than the green but can still pack a punch. Great uses for the jalapeño are in fresh salsa, stews, or potato salads. When the jalepeño is dried and smoked, it is known as a "chipotle." Just a little chipotle goes a long way in providing both heat (5+ rating) and a wonderful smoky flavor in stews, soups, mashed potatoes, and, oh yeah, chili.

Japones: (ha-pon-es) This little red chile is usually found in its dried form. It is most commonly sold as red chile flakes and used on pizza, Italian food, and in salsas made from ground, dried chiles. It can also be used to perk up soups and stews. Rates a 6 on the heat scale.

New Mexico: This chile is available fresh in both its unripe green and ripened red form. Also known as "Hatch chiles," they form the basis of many green chile sauces as well as molè verde. It is the most common chile used for making chile rellenos (stuffed chiles). With a thick skin that chars easily, this chile can easily be roasted, skinned, and stuffed with a variety of fillings or puréed for use in soups, stews, and sauces. It is also used in its dried form. Depending on the ripeness of the chile when it was dried, it is also known as "chile colorado" or "colored chile." As one of the predominant dried chiles used in Mexican cooking, it is advisable to get acquainted with this chile in both its fresh and dried forms. Heat rating of 5 or less.

Pequín: (pay-keen or peh-keen) A very small oval chile often picked in the wild; when they are cultivated they lose some of their flavor and heat. It is a cousin to the tepín, which is also a wild chile but is round in shape. They are used in both fresh and dried forms in chilito, salsa, and soups. This is one of the more expensive chiles, both dried and fresh, since it must be hand-gathered in the desert. Heat rating of 8.5.

Poblano: (po-blan-oh) also known as a "fresh pasilla." The poblano chile is considered the workhorse of peppers; it has the thickest flesh and skin. Fresh, it is available both green and deep red when fully ripe. This chile is mild in heat with a rating of 3, but long in flavor. It can be used raw as a replacement or embellishment for green bell peppers in any dish. For a real treat, use it in meatloaf or in stuffings. This pepper is the backbone for recipes such as tortilla soup and green chile sauces and is used as a replacement for New Mexico or Anaheim chiles in chile rellenos (stuffed chiles). The real wonder of this chile is in its dried forms. If the chile is picked while still green and then dried, it turns very dark, almost black. Dried it is known as "ancho negro," "mulato," or "pasilla"; the flavors of the ancho negro are grassy, slightly bitter, tobacco-like and leatherlike. If allowed to ripen on the vine, then dried, this pepper is known as "ancho rojo," with an earthy, sweet, and slightly smoky flavor. Both the dried green and dried red poblanos are used in red chile or mole sauces.

Pulla or **puya:** (poo-ya) Thinner and slightly shorter than the guajillo, these thin-fleshed chiles have sharp fruit flavors with a fairly high heat rating (6). Often used in chili and sauces.

Scotch bonnet: This kissing cousin to the habanero has a much more citrusy and tropical scent and flavor than the habanero, although they both are at the top end of the heat scale at 10. Trying to cook Caribbean foods or jerk seasoning with habaneros instead of Scotch bonnets is just not the same, but they will do in a pinch. The citrus flavor lends itself to sauces paired with grilled seafood or poultry. It can also be used in soups, like pepper-pot, or tropical fruit salsas.

Serrano: (sir-on-oh) About half the size of the jalapeño but packed with flavor and heat, with a rating of 7. In Mexico, the most popular use of this chile is in salsas, both fresh and cooked. It is often called for in mole verdes and green sauces. This chile has about twice the bite of the jalapeño but also has a pleasing fresh flavor; this flavor carries through when it is cooked. Red and fully ripe serranos are slightly sweet. Both forms of this pepper are used in Thai, Indian, Indonesian and Middle-Eastern dishes as well as in fresh and cooked salsas and pickled in brine.

Tabasco: The sauce (McIlhenny Tabasco) from this small fresh chile is probably the genesis of all chileheads. It is a small greenish yellow to orange red chile, transplanted from the Tabasco region of Mexico to Louisiana. It is a little shorter than the serrano, with a stronger punch, rating a 9. It has a green onion flavor and a brilliant burn. This is a great addition to the gumbo pot, jambalaya, or pepper vinegar.

Tepín: (ta-peen) Also known as "chiltepín" or "chilecpín," this small, round, and bright red chile is a cousin of the pequín. Both are known as "wild" chiles, picked from plants that grow in the wild; if cultivated they do not have the desired flavor or punch. These chiles are used in both fresh and dried forms in chilito, salsas, and soups, and pickled and bottled in jars or cans. Heat rating of 8.5.

Thai: If you have ever eaten at a Thai restaurant, you're familiar with the power these small fresh chiles have. They come in a range of colors from green, yellow, and orange to red and have a heat that seems to linger longer than most chiles. With a heat rating of 7 to 8, they are used in soup dishes, cooked with rice, and featured in just about every type of meat dish. This chile pairs well with peanut butter sauces and coconut.

Yellow wax or **güero:** (wed-oh) Also known as the blond banana, Santa Fe or Hungarian wax chile. It is a medium-sized fresh chile that ranges in color from an almost white, pale yellow to medium yellow. This chile has mild flowery flavor with a thin but juicy flesh and is great when used in fresh salsas or when charred. It is also used in soups and in sauces for its flavor. Heat rating of 3.

Hot Sauce Guide

Cool Cayenne Pepper Sauce: This is an all purpose Louisiana-style sauce.

Crazy Caribbean Sauce: This is a Central American-style sauce. Fresh habaneros, limes, and carrots are the keys to this sauce's great flavor.

Garlic-Chile Sauce: Many people have said that this is the best hot sauce that we produce. It is similar to sriracha sauce which is named after a fishing village in Thailand. The sauce has a medium heat and a fresh chile flavor.

Ginger Peach Hot Sauce: Is there a hot sauce that it is good on ice cream? This is the one that you should try on your pork, chicken, fish, or vanilla ice cream.

Hurtin Jalapeño Sauce: Chayote and jalapeños combine to make a unusually tasty, spicy sauce.

Hurtin' Habanero Sauce: This sauce has a distinct habanero and spice flavor. With a definite punch, this sauce is one of our best selling items.

Insane Mary Mix: This mix is loaded with pepper and Worcestershire and herbs and chiles. It is a thick and full of flavor. Just add vodka or drink it instead of V8.

Insanity Limited Edition Reserve: My hottest product. I only make one special batch of this sauce per year. Every bottle is hand signed, numbered, and dated. It is packaged in a wooden coffin and wrapped in caution tape.

Insanity Sauce: This is the sauce that created the whole super hot sauce category. After ten years, this is still my best selling product. Everyone should try it at least once.

Insanity Spice: For those who find that regular habanero and red savina chiles are not quite hot enough, we have spiked our dry seasoning to make it even hotter. Be careful.

Insanity Steak Sauce: If you want a bold steak sauce whose flavor leaps up and smacks you, then you must try this sauce.

Jammin' Jerk Sauce: This sauce will get your goat. Prepare your jerk pit and pour some of this delicious sauce on your grilled meat.

Jump Up and Kiss Me Smoky Chipotle Sauce: This sauce combines the wonderful smoky flavor of chipotle chiles with dutch cocoa and a number of other savory spices. The flavor of your pork or chicken will jump up and kiss you.

Soyabi Sauce: Soy plus wasabi is soyabi, but not without adding ginger, garlic, and a special imported sesame oil. Your salmon, tuna, and chicken will never be the same.

Temporary Insanity Hot Sauce: This sauce is Insanity Sauce with about a quarter of the heat.

Total Insanity Sauce: This is a garlic-lime-chile flavored sauce with about half the heat of Insanity Sauce. It is also my personal favorite among our super hot sauces.

Ultimate Insanity Sauce: This is our hottest product. It may be more effective as an industrial cleanser than a sauce.

I have many other products including the three-time gold medal winners at the Worldwide Mustard Competition: Hurtin' Habanero and Honey Mustard. My other products include: Organic Red Heirloom Pasta Sauce, Organic Roasted Garlic and Sweet Basil Sauce, Golden Heirloom Pasta Sauce, Wild Mushroom Sauce, Original Bloody Mary Mix, Mango Margarita, Insanity Mustard, Jalabeaños, Olives in Pain, Badlands Barbecue Sauce, Garlic-Chile Sauce, Soyabi Sauce, Original Steak Sauce, Insanity Steak Sauce, Insanity Salsa, Insanity Corn, Dave's Burning Nuts, Dave's Painful Pretzels, Insanity Snax, Insanity Beef Sticks, Dave's 6 Pure Dried Chiles, and a Chilehead Survival Kit. In my Jump Up and Kiss Me Line, I have a papaya sauce, and a passionfruit sauce.

To find information on or to purchase any of these products you can call 800-758-0372 or visit www.davesgourmet.com.

Index